PRAISE

"*Accompanying* is inspiring and humbling to all who think we know and have a strategy to craft a better society. This stirring work shows us that solidarity is not an abstract strategy requiring a professional party leading the way to consolidate working class power."
— Immanuel Ness, editor of *Working USA* and coeditor of *Ours to Master and to Own: Workers' Control from the Commune to the Present*

"*Accompanying* is a concept, a way of living, central to some of the best radical work the world over, one that opens up new possibilities for human liberation. Lynd's delineation of accompanying is one that activists will do well to examine. It will benefit anyone wishing to live a life of meaning for the benefit of the underprivileged who strive always for a better world, and for the ongoing efforts to create that world."
— Andy Piascik, former staff member of the League for Industrial Democracy

"*Accompanying* is arguably the most thoughtful examination of Archbishop Oscar Romero's concept of accompaniment insofar as it helps us to understand how liberation theology matured from taking a 'preferential option for the poor' to companionship with the poor as they organize themselves. This legacy flows into the Occupy Movement today when it reclaims foreclosed homes, and occupies banks and spaces collectively and spontaneously. This book would be important at any moment in history, but is indispensable today as we accompany one another in the quest to free ourselves from the shackles of the world the 1 percent has inflicted on us."
— Carl Mirra, author of *The Admirable Radical: Staughton Lynd and Cold War Dissent, 1945–1970*

"Everything that Staughton Lynd writes is original and provocative. This little book is no exception. Among his greatest contributions on display here is the transformation of the 'organizer' and 'organized' into a collaboration of different people with different skills, each making a decisive contribution."
— Paul Buhle, author of *Robin Hood: People's Outlaw and Forest Hero*

"Staughton and Alice Lynd's theory and practice of accompaniment as set forth in this book represents a major contribution to understanding how activists should work for social change."
— Jules Lobel, president, Center for Constitutional Rights and author of *Success Without Victory: The Long Road to Justice in America*

Accompanying
Pathways to Social Change

Staughton Lynd

ISBN: 978-1-60486-666-7
LCCN: 2012913636

Cover design by John Yates/stealworks.com
Interior design by Jonathan Rowland

PM Press
PO Box 23912
Oakland, CA 94623
www.pmpress.org

10 9 8 7 6 5 4 3 2 1

Printed on recycled paper by the Employee Owners of Thom-
son-Shore in Dexter, Michigan.
www.thomsonshore.com

Contents

Introduction

THIS LITTLE BOOK OFFERS A SINGLE SIMPLE THESIS.

I believe that most (not all) of the movements of the 1960s suffered from a mistaken and superficial conception of social change that we called "organizing."

In what follows, I will discuss many aspects of this organizing model. For the moment, think of it as a process whereby person A decides what it would be desirable for person B to think and do, and then seeks to bring about that predetermined result.

Why do I call this idea of organizing mistaken and superficial? Because, as I shall seek to show, the result is either (as in the labor movement) a complex and restrictive institutional environment that stands in the way of creative and spontaneous action from below, or (in the heartbreaking case of the civil rights movement) a situation such that when the organizer leaves, some of the worst aspects of the way things were before reassert themselves.

Is there an alternative, a different practice, a new vision toward which young people who wish to change the world in fundamental ways might turn? I believe that there is. It is called "accompaniment."

Dr. Paul Farmer on "Accompaniment"

The idea of accompaniment has lately begun to attract attention in the United States.

On May 25, 2011, for example, Dr. Paul Farmer delivered a commencement address at Harvard University's Kennedy School of Government called "Accompaniment as Policy." In the course of his address, reproduced by the Office of the Special Envoy for Haiti, by my count Farmer used the French noun "*accompagnateur*" (one who accompanies) seven times, the verb "accompany" eight times, and the noun "accompaniment" thirty-seven times.

What did Dr. Farmer mean by these fifty-two words?

In 2003, a biography of Dr. Farmer had appeared with the title *Mountains Beyond Mountains*.[1] This much-acclaimed book had some-

---

1. Tracy Kidder, *Mountains Beyond Mountains* (New York: Random House, 2003).

what the aspect of a victory lap for Farmer and the organization he cofounded, Partners In Health. Then, of course, came the Haitian earthquake, validating the proverb that author Tracy Kidder chose for the title: beyond each mountain range there is another; or, stated differently, as you solve one problem, another presents itself.

Dr. Farmer makes clear in the first paragraph of his Harvard talk that the aftermath of the Haitian earthquake was for him an object lesson about the arena he thought he knew most about. In discussing the things he learned and relearned during these difficult years, he states that "[a]ll of them turn about the notion of accompaniment." The word "accompaniment" is an elastic one: "it means just what you'd imagine, and more. *To accompany someone is to go somewhere with him or her, to break bread together, to be present on a journey with a beginning and an end.*" Farmer indicates that we're almost never sure about the end.

> There's an element of mystery, of openness, in accompaniment. I'll go with you and support you on your journey wherever it leads. I'll keep you company and share your fate for a while. And by "a while," I don't mean a little while. Accompaniment is much more about sticking with a task until it's deemed completed by the person or people being accompanied, rather than by the *accompagnateur*.[2]

The rest of this remarkable paper consists of illustrations of "accompaniment" from Dr. Farmer's rich and varied experience. One such illustration has to do with a certain windswept plain north of Port-au-Prince that had been identified as a possible resettlement location for earthquake victims. Scores of architects and urban planners set to work on plans for the site. Nobody bothered to go there. Had they done so, they would have learned that the location was in the middle of a floodplain and anything built there would have sunk into the mud during the rainy season. The lesson, according to Farmer, is "the necessity of physical proximity to accompaniment." He reminds us that the Latin roots of "accompaniment" refer to being together ("com") in eating bread ("panis"), face to face.

---

2. Paul Farmer, "Accompaniment as Policy" (Office of the Special Envoy for Haiti, 2011), p. 1.

Occupy Wall Street and Accompaniment

Occupy Wall Street, itself inspired partly by initiatives on other continents, gave rise to parallel uprisings all over the United States and then all over the world. Occupy Wall Street illustrates additional aspects of accompaniment.

Occupy Wall Street and its progeny reinforce the idea of equality between individuals and groups in bringing about social change. There is no "vanguard party." There is no "lead organizer." There is not even the notion of a particular class or social grouping as the initiator of change. In place of the verticalism characteristic of past radical scenarios, the practice of Occupiers is endlessly horizontal.

The horizontalism of Occupy Wall Street is consistent with what my wife and I have come to practice over the years. We found our way to accompaniment by way of Alice's experience of draft counseling. She experienced draft counseling as an encounter of "two experts."[3] The draft counselor was presumably an expert on Selective Service law and regulations, and on the practice of local draft boards. But the counselee was an expert on his own life experience, on the predictable responses of parents and significant others, and on how much risk the counselee was prepared to confront.

I describe in the chapter on the labor movement how, as a historian, I derived my interpretation of what has gone wrong with the trade union movement from steelworkers John Sargent and Ed Mann, and automobile worker Marty Glaberman. They turned upside-down conventional praise for the "workplace contractualism" introduced by the Congress of Industrial Organizations (CIO).

As lawyers, both Alice and I have repeatedly drawn on the expertise of our clients. We may have at our fingertips the language of the National Labor Relations Act, the procedures of the National Labor Relations Board, and comparable information about other statutes and administrative agencies. But our clients understood the dynamics of their particular shop floors better than we ever could. If the clients were from a unionized workplace and worked under a collective bargaining agreement, they were likely to know how it had been interpreted and thus be at least as accurate as ourselves in predicting the fate of any particular grievance. In the U.S. Steel

---

3. See the chapter on the antiwar movement in this book, and Alice Lynd and Staughton Lynd, *Stepping Stones: Memoir of a Life Together* (Lanham, MD: Lexington Books, 2009), pp. 84–87.

case, the workers suggested the theory of our litigation: the company had promised that as long as its Youngstown, Ohio, facilities were operating at a profit, they would remain open.[4] Similarly, when Alice represented persons seeking Social Security disability benefits, only they could describe the loss of life functions imposed by their impairments. Thus, the language of "accompaniment" that we later became acquainted with in Central America described a process we had already come to know in practice.

The idea of accompaniment developed in two stages. Initially formulated as a "preferential option for the poor," the idea implicitly assumed that he or she who exercised that option was a middle-class religious personage or intellectual responding to the needs of the less fortunate.

But if accompanier and accompanied are conceptualized, not as one person assisting another person in need, but as two experts, the intellectual universe is transformed. No longer do we have one kind of person helping a person of another kind. Instead we have two persons exploring the way forward together. Oscar Romero, Archbishop of El Salvador, may have been the first to use the word "accompaniment" to describe such a relationship.

Marxism and liberation theology have accustomed us to think of working people, or the poor, as the essential protagonists of social change. Occupy Wall Street offers a different paradigm. The typical participant is a young person who got a high school diploma, completed college or, in some cases, graduate school, is burdened by student debts, and can't get a job. Only after students or former students had carried out the initial direct action were they joined by members of various New York City trade unions.

This is a pattern that I have found in other uprisings often assumed to have been revolts initiated by the working class. In Russia in 1904–1905, in Hungary in 1956, in France in 1968, students acted before workers, but when workers intervened in support of students or against the same enemies, rebellion turned into potential revolution.[5] The vision is of an entire people—the "99 percent" excluded from wealth and power—joining together to change the world.

---

4. *Local 1330, et al. v. U.S. Steel*, 492 F.Supp. 1 (N.D. Ohio 1980), *aff'd in part and rev'd in part*, 631 F.2d 1264 (6th Cir. 1980).
5. Staughton Lynd, "Students and Workers in the Transition to Socialism," in *From Here to There: The Staughton Lynd Reader*, ed. Andrej Grubačić (Oakland, CA: PM Press, 2010), pp. 219–27.

Some Things That Accompaniment Is Not

Before I plunge into specifics, let me anticipate certain objections and try to respond to those concerns.

First, I do not propose a mechanical, externally defined understanding of what it means to "accompany." For example, the Center for Constitutional Rights has performed wonders for the "enemy combatants" imprisoned at Guantánamo, and my wife and I have formed deep relationships of trust with prisoners at Ohio's supermaximum security prison. But self-evidently neither staff at the Center, nor Alice and I, are incarcerated in one of these formidable prisons. Nonetheless, we have been able significantly to share the journey-in-place of those confined there. (Accompanying has been easier for Alice and me because Ohio's "supermax" is located less than half an hour's drive from our home.)

Thus accompanying means something more than going to a place where there are poor people and staying there a long time. There are industrial workers who as young radicals in the 1930s "colonized" (to use the word then in vogue) by moving to Detroit, or to Gary, Indiana, and stayed there for the rest of their lives. They did not necessarily move the larger society one step closer to a qualitatively different one. Some of them ended up writing campaign literature for far less radical automobile workers or steelworkers in local union elections.

Also, as noted at the outset, I don't mean to suggest that all the movements and organizations of the 1960s practiced "organizing" rather than "accompaniment." Certain currents within the women's movement present a notable exception. For instance, our friend from Spelman College and Mississippi Summer, Chude (Pam) Allen, wrote a striking pamphlet about egalitarian consciousness-raising groups in the early women's movement, entitled "Free Space." Similarly, in the "We Won't Go" movement made up of men who refused to serve in Vietnam, the group at Cornell University agreed that there would not be a single "lead organizer." Instead, each person who became involved was responsible for approaching other possible recruits: "We finally agreed that each of us would talk to one or two other people, discuss the idea with them and then all meet together in a week. In this way, all four of us were now organizers."[6]

---

6. Tom Bell, "Organizing Draft Resistance," in *We Won't Go: Personal Accounts of War Objectors*, ed. Alice Lynd (Boston: Beacon Press, 1968), p. 209.

Indeed, along with the organizing schema that was dominant on the Left in the 1960s, there also existed the practice of leading by example. There is an inwardness to both individual exemplary action and accompaniment that sets them apart from trade union organizing and the formation of "community organizations" by followers of Saul Alinsky. Thus Rosa Parks in Montgomery, the four students who sat-in at Greensboro, and the students who continued the Freedom Rides from Alabama into Mississippi, did their "messaging" by example, without knowing what results (if any) their activity would produce. Likewise Bob Moses went to Mississippi by himself, an act of personal courage. On the basis of conversation with local African-American leaders, surely an expression of accompaniment, he adopted a strategy of voter registration. At a subsequent meeting of Student Nonviolent Coordinating Committee (SNCC) staff at the Highlander Folk School, the relative merits of a voter registration strategy and a "direct action" strategy aimed at public accommodations (like lunch counter sit-ins and freedom rides) were hotly debated. But after the group decided to pursue both strategies, it turned out that attempting voter registration in the Deep South amounted to a form of direct action, with all the same risks!

I experienced this confluence of accompaniment and exemplary action in making an unauthorized trip to Hanoi in December 1965, together with Tom Hayden and Herbert Aptheker. We were acting out the idea of personal contact between the people of warring nations, at some personal risk. That was exemplary action. But once in North Vietnam, we met and talked with a captured U.S. pilot, and visitors who came after us like Howard Zinn and Father Daniel Berrigan actually accompanied such pilots back to the United States.

I also wish to respond to what I anticipate may be the first reaction of some readers: "Oh, this is just Staughton's warmed-over version of liberation theology." This is wrong for several reasons.

As suggested above, Gustavo Gutierrez and Oscar Romero represented different stages in the development of liberation theology. The preferential option for the poor, presented in the late 1960s by Gutierrez, had a good deal in common with traditional notions of Christian charity. The works of mercy outlined in Matthew chapter 25 were visiting the sick and those in prison, sheltering the homeless, and feeding the hungry. Romero, I hope to show, was a man from a poor family who in the late 1970s shifted emphasis from helping the poor to listening to them and learning from their experience.

Also, I have come to feel that liberation theology as an interpretation of the New Testament and the life of Jesus is open to serious question. In the Church of St. Mary of the Angels in Managua, that Alice and I attended during several brief stays in Sandinista Nicaragua, the liturgy was the Missa Campesina, or peasants' mass. A portion of the mass presents Jesus as a day laborer, hot and dirty, standing in line with other workers at the end of the week to receive his wages.

Yet the parables of Jesus repeatedly view the world through the eyes of absentee landlords, employers, or masters, dealing with subordinates who work for them. In one such parable, part of all three Synoptic Gospels and the earlier Gospel of Thomas, an absentee landlord who owns a vineyard sends messengers to collect rent from his tenants.[7] The first two messengers or groups of messengers are badly beaten or killed. The landlord then sends his "beloved" son who is murdered. Who is this beloved son? Is he the Jesus who stands in line with other laborers at the end of the week to be paid?

Finally, accompaniment could be portrayed as the ultimate opportunism: the activist, it might be suggested, does whatever "local people" consider desirable, from lynching to armed insurrection. Monseñor Romero faced this problem in El Salvador in the late 1970s and we will explore it in detail when we come to consider his life and teaching. For now, it may be enough to say: no, the *accompagnateur* and the person accompanied are equals; each brings to their encounter a particular expertise based on professional training or life experience and as they come to form through their shared experience a vision of a better world, each has an obligation to be faithful to that dream.

Special Thanks

I want to offer special thanks to four persons: Alice Lynd, Jules Lobel, Andrej Grubačić, and Denis O'Hearn.

Alice deserves all the usual things that authors express to spouses who accompanied them while a book was being written. But Alice deserves far more.

The entire conception of "accompaniment" in our experience springs from Alice's years as a draft counselor, and her formulation of

---

7. The different versions of this parable appear in Matthew 21:33–41; Mark 12:1–9; Luke 20:9–16.

the idea of "two experts." Because of her insight, we practiced this idea not only in Alice's draft counseling, but also in oral history and legal representation that we undertook together, before we encountered the word "accompaniment" on visits to Latin America in the 1980s.

As will be obvious to the reader, Alice contributed to the chapters on war resistance and uprisings of prisoners. While this book was being written, Alice was also researching and writing an article, "Unfair and Can't Be Fixed: The Machinery of Death in Ohio," accepted for publication by the *University of Toledo Law Review* in fall of 2012.

Jules Lobel is a professor of constitutional law, international law, and civil rights law at the University of Pittsburgh School of Law, and, at the time of this writing, president of the Center for Constitutional Rights. He, Alice, and I made up the core of the legal team that took to the U.S. Supreme Court a class action concerning conditions of confinement at Ohio's supermaximum security prison, where prisoners alleged to be the "worst of the worst" are kept in solitary confinement at least twenty-three hours a day. Jules argued the case in the Supreme Court and we succeeded in establishing fundamental due process rights for prisoners threatened with years of isolation at the Ohio State Penitentiary.

Initially, Jules and I envisioned a single book that we would write together. The problem we sought to confront was how to embody visionary impulses from below such as the labor sit-ins of the 1930s or the civil rights movement of the 1960s in an ongoing network of radical institutions. As our research and dialogue proceeded the idea surfaced that there should be two books: first, this short discussion of the phenomenon with which I was preoccupied, Archbishop Romero's idea of accompaniment; and then, hopefully, a second book addressing the larger question of the transition from capitalism to socialism. All three of us—Jules, Alice, and I—look forward to this continuing collaboration.

Andrej Grubačić is a Yugoslav exile immersed in the recent worldwide movement that calls itself "anarchist." Together, he and I have produced an extended conversation about the needed synthesis of Marxist and anarchist traditions, and a collection of my fugitive writings with a comprehensive introduction by Andrej.[8] This book,

---

8. Staughton Lynd and Andrej Grubačić, *Wobblies and Zapatistas: Conversations on Anarchism, Marxism, and Radical History* (Oakland, CA: PM Press, 2008); Andrej Grubačić, "Introduction," in *From Here to There*, pp. 3–26.

like everything I have thought about in recent years, has benefited from his critical comments.

Finally, there is Denis O'Hearn, author of an account of the hunger strike by Bobby Sands and other Irish political prisoners in which Sands and nine of his comrades died.[9] Copies of Denis's book reached prisoners held in indefinite solitary confinement at California's supermaximum security prison at Pelican Bay. Their successful hunger strike is described later in this book. Prisoners at the heart of the insurgency say that had they not read Denis's book, along with writings on Mayan cosmology, they would never have gotten the idea that they could proceed on a course of peaceful resistance through a hunger strike and they would never have achieved their victory.

Niles, Ohio
December 2011

---

9. Denis O'Hearn, *Nothing but an Unfinished Song: Bobby Sands, the Irish Hunger Striker Who Ignited a Generation* (New York: Nation Books, 2006).

Organizing

The Labor Movement

AS A HISTORIAN AND AS A LAWYER SPECIALIZING IN EMPLOYMENT law, I had continuing contact with rank-and-file workers and union organizing in Chicago, Youngstown, and Pittsburgh for more than thirty years, beginning in 1967. It was a profound experience of accompanying. I learned that what a middle-class professional like me can offer is needed and important, but even more significant is the way that workers like Vicky Starr, John Sargent, and Ed Mann accompany each other.

The concept of "organizing" in the United States derives from the trade union movement. Viewers of the movie *Norma Rae* will recall the essentials. The full-time "organizer," whose salary is paid by a national union, is sent into town and registers at a motel. The organizer seeks to win recognition from a local employer at a designated workplace as the exclusive bargaining representative of the workers.

The time this process is expected to take depends on whether the workplace has been characterized by the union as "hot" or "cold." The organizer proceeds as quickly as possible. He or she—usually he—gets to know activists at the plant to whom other workers look for informal leadership. A committee of such activists is formed, and potential union support in different parts of the workplace is carefully evaluated. After a few weeks or months, the organizing effort "goes public." Supporters are encouraged to wear union buttons to work. Cards indicating a desire to join the union, or to hold an election, are circulated. When the number of signatures is well over half of eligible workers at the targeted shop or office, the employer is approached with the demand for a "card check" assessment of union support by a neutral party (often in exchange for a weak collective bargaining agreement). Alternatively, the National Labor Relations Board may be asked to conduct an election, as in *Norma Rae*.

The aftermath of this process was not shown in the movie. Typically, the day after the election, win or lose, the organizer checks out of the motel and leaves town. If the union has been unable to obtain employer recognition, workers who made known their pro-union sentiments by wearing buttons or circulating cards are left exposed to retaliation. If the union has won the election, other representatives of the national union often show up with a predetermined collective bargaining agreement. Contract proposals appropriate to the local situation may be ignored.

This (of course with many variations) has been the story of union organizing in the United States since the 1930s.[1]

Community organizer Saul Alinsky did his initial work "Back of the Yards" in southwest Chicago. He modeled his organizing on that of the CIO packinghouse workers' union, which was in process of formation there. I became one of the first four staff members of Mr. Alinsky's Industrial Areas Foundation Training Institute in 1968. I believe I have a basis for the conclusion that union organizing and community organizing à la Alinsky are cut from the same cloth. There is the same tendency to personalize conflict by singling out a principal spokesperson for the "enemy" by name. There is the same conviction that support can be mobilized only by appealing to the narrow, self-interested motives of individual workers. There is the same expectation that once the fledgling union or community organization has been recognized as a negotiating partner, all concerned will put their feet on the table and break out the liquor and cigars. An exaggerated atmosphere of hostility is followed by an artificial atmosphere of good feeling.

As I will explain, members of the Students for a Democratic Society (SDS) who in the 1960s took up residence in city neighborhoods in an effort to create an "interracial movement of the poor" pursued a similar game plan. It was never the intention of these would-be organizers to stay in a neighborhood for what Dr. Farmer would consider more than "a little while." Instead, after a few months or, for the most persistent, a few years, SDS organizers like trade union organizers departed the scene and moved on.

The organizing model sketched in the preceding paragraphs is presently in crisis. Trade union membership, about one-third of the work force just after World War II, is now approximately 10 percent. Since the 1970s corporations have moved manufacturing out of the United States on a massive scale to take advantage of lower wage rates elsewhere. No longer insistent on equal pay for equal work,

---

1. Once in a while, workers form a union without the help of outside organizers. This was essentially what happened when a group of visiting nurses in Youngstown created "Visiting Nurses Solidarity." See Lynd and Lynd, *Stepping Stones*, pp. 122–24.

unions have agreed to collective bargaining contracts that provide two or more wage scales for the same job. The vision of dramatic social change in the direction of a more democratic workplace has given way to a situation in which, when the company announces the impending shutdown of a plant, American trade unions stand by helplessly.

The question presents itself: can the labor movement still hope to lead the whole society toward what Youngstown steelworker Ed Mann called "a better way." This question can be broken down into two more specific questions, one looking backward and the other forward.

1. Why Did the Congress of Industrial Organizations So Rapidly Abandon the Shopfloor Self-Activity and Political Radicalism That Characterized Its Beginnings?

When my wife Alice and I moved to Chicago in 1967, the student movement was turning toward a strategy of imagined working-class revolution. Working-class young men were being drafted to fight in Vietnam and beginning to resist the orders of their officers. As in the 1930s, many middle-class young people were leaving the campus to become steelworkers or workers in automobile assembly plants.

Hoping to evaluate the prospects of working-class radicalism, Alice and I sought to explore the world of working-class experience, first in Chicago from 1967 to 1976, and then in Youngstown and Pittsburgh, from 1976 to the late 1990s. (We are still in Ohio but, Youngstown having substituted prisons for steel mills, we have become advocates for prisoners.) "Go see so-and-so," we would be told, and led in this way from one person to the next we put together a collection of oral histories entitled *Rank and File*. We created occasions when veterans of the labor movement of the 1930s could share what they had learned with the new generation of would-be radicals. We helped to organize a Writers' Workshop in Gary where a variety of people told their stories.

What we found was fundamentally at odds with the conception of working-class consciousness as inherently retrospective, defensive, and pragmatic. For example, Vicky Starr was a child of Eastern European immigrants who grew up on a farm in Michigan. Vicky's father had been a coal miner and had "bought a few books about Lenin and Gorky." She recalled that when Sacco and Vanzetti were executed "the foreign-born people were in mourning for a week."

The family practiced what Vicky's father described as a socialist idea: "No work, no eat." Vicky went on to help to organize the Packinghouse Workers of America in South Chicago and, after World War II, secretaries at the University of Chicago. She described herself as a socialist throughout her adult life.[2]

Vicky introduced us to two friends and fellow spirits, Sylvia Woods and Katherine Hyndman, and the three became the protagonists of the documentary movie *Union Maids*. Sylvia, an African American, came from New Orleans, where her father was a skilled roofer and a member of Marcus Garvey's Back to Africa movement. After moving to Chicago, Sylvia helped to organize a United Automobile Workers (UAW) local union at Bendix during World War II. Memorably, she stated in her interview in *Rank and File*, "We never had [dues] check-off. We didn't want it. We said if you have a closed shop and check-off, everybody sits on their butts and they don't have to worry about organizing and they don't care what happens. We never wanted it."

Sylvia became a radical when she met white workers who fought for equal rights for black workers. They turned out to be Communists.[3]

The third union maid, Katherine Hyndman, appeared in *Rank and File* under the name Christine Ellis. Kate stated at the end of *Union Maids*, "I still believe in socialism, but I don't know if there is any single European country that has the kind of socialism that I would want. To me, socialism should mean that the greatest say-so is the people themselves. Let the people decide."

To be sure, the union maids were not typical, any more than Tom Paine was typical of artisans at the time of the American Revolution. What they prove, however, is that working-class radicalism remains a possibility. In time of crisis, such a possibility can spread like a spark from one person to the next and turn into a wildfire.

So what happened to the socialist radicalism espoused by workers like Vicky Starr, Sylvia Woods and Kate Hyndman in Chicago and

---

2. Vicky Starr, "Back of the Yards," in *Rank and File: Personal Histories by Working-Class Organizers*, ed. Alice and Staughton Lynd (expanded edition, Chicago: Haymarket Books, 2011), pp. 67–88, and "Organizing White-Collar Workers," ibid., pp. 297–304.
3. Sylvia Woods, "You Have to Fight for Freedom," in *Rank and File*, ed. Lynd and Lynd (expanded edition), pp. 111–29.

northern Indiana, or (as will appear) by Ed Mann and John Barbero in Youngstown? Why did the CIO become a movement that caused Gary, Indiana, steelworker Jesse Reese to cry out, "Your dog don't bark no more"?[4] How did the new trade union movement become a top-down, bureaucratic affair that caused me to describe rank-and-file labor activists in Youngstown as "broken-hearted lovers"?

Many answers to these questions have been offered. The labor movement's current distress has been ascribed to the National Labor Relations Act (the NLRA, or Wagner Act) of 1935; to the Supreme Court's restrictive interpretation of the NLRA in the years immediately following the law's enactment; to passage of the Taft-Hartley Act in 1947; to the expulsion of Communist-led unions from the Congress of Industrial Organizations; to the lackluster leadership of the labor movement following the merger of the CIO and AF of L; and to the influence of business ideology on the courts and National Labor Relations Board (NLRB) in recent decades.

I have come to feel that these were secondary causes or symptoms. The heart of the matter, I gradually concluded, lay elsewhere. Let me explain.

Growing up in the 1930s and 1940s with liberal, Left-leaning parents, I had absorbed a view of the labor movement still affirmed by most labor historians, labor lawyers, and labor organizers. It was taken for granted that the creation of the Congress of Industrial Organizations was a Good Thing. There were books on the shelves of our family's apartment with titles like *Labor on the March*. The objective of all non-unionized workers was assumed to be employer recognition of a single union as exclusive bargaining agent, with periodic negotiation of comprehensive collective bargaining contracts.

Hope was expressed that a labor party might soon come into being, as in Great Britain.

My father voted for the American Labor Party in several New York state elections. In January 1949, he gave a speech at the Fourth Annual International Educational Conference of the UAW-CIO in Milwaukee. The union printed the talk as a pamphlet after (according to a prefatory note by Victor Reuther) "reports of it . . . circulated through the union with the result that there has been an insistent demand for its publication." My dad closed his speech by saying

---

4. George Patterson, Jesse Reese, and John Sargent, "Your Dog Don't Bark No More," in *Rank and File*, ed. Lynd and Lynd (expanded edition), pp. 103–5.

that this was a period like the shift from feudalism to capitalism five hundred years ago. He thought that "liberal democracy" was a compromise between democracy and capitalism that was "finished," and that we were going to have either a great deal more democracy or a great deal less. He ended by affirming that "labor looks to me like the only force in contemporary society big enough and strong enough to save democracy for us Americans."

I had never seen such happiness in my father's face as when he came through the front door of our apartment after giving that talk.

However, two events in my childhood raised some question about organized labor's presumed democratic mission.

The first was reading a book called *The Managerial Revolution* by an ex-Trotskyist named James Burnham. Burnham said that in the transition from feudalism to capitalism, the middle class, before it took state power, had created a network of new institutions within the shell or womb of feudal society: free cities, guilds, Protestant congregations, corporations, ultimately parliaments. Nothing like this was possible within the more tightly woven fabric of capitalism, Burnham argued. Marx, he noted, had expected trade unions to become the counterparts of medieval communes. But the reality was that while trade unions may soften some of capitalism's hardships, they did not prefigure a new society but were part of the existing scheme of things.

A second discordant note was sounded in a book by C. Wright Mills called *The New Men of Power* about the full-time officers and staff of CIO unions. As I glanced through the book, I saw that it began with a quotation about a 1916 incident involving members of the Industrial Workers of the World (IWW). They had rented a barge called the *Verona* to take them to a free speech fight in the West Coast city of Everett, Washington. As the barge approached the dock the sheriff called out, "Who are your leaders?" From the ship came the response, "We are all leaders." The sheriff thereupon ordered those under his command to open fire. "We are all leaders" was an alternative image of what a union could be like.

It was not until Alice and I moved to Chicago that I began to experience enlightenment with regard to the question: what happened to the radicalism of the early CIO? It came about through dramatic encounters with a steelworker, John Sargent, and an automobile worker, Marty Glaberman.

John Sargent

At about the same time Alice and I were getting to know the "union maids," I had the opportunity to meet steelworker John Sargent. Soon after our first meeting, John invited Alice, me, and our three-year-old daughter Martha for dinner. Almost the first thing he did when we arrived was to take our daughter by the hand to show her the goldfish in a little pond in his back yard. It was the same quality of empathy described to me by a steelworker who told how, at a gathering of rank and filers, John put his arm around one of the many Mexican immigrants who worked at the mill and spoke glowingly of the man's contributions to the cause. "That man seemed to grow a foot taller as Sargent spoke," I was told.

John Sargent was the first president of the eighteen-thousand-member local union at Inland Steel in East Chicago, Indiana, in the late 1930s. He was reelected in 1943, 1944, 1946, and, despite vicious Red-baiting, 1964. When we met him, he was again working as an electrician in the mill.

In her oral history, Vicky Starr had described working-class self-activity in Chicago packinghouses in the late 1930s. John Sargent, in a presentation to a community forum on "Labor History from the Standpoint of the Rank and File," narrated very similar events during those same years at Inland Steel. In neither setting was there a written collective bargaining agreement, but in both situations workers took direct action in response to an unjust discharge or a unilateral change in conditions, and achieved results. When the war came, Vicky left her work in packing but John remained a steelworker for another thirty years. Accordingly, John had an opportunity to contrast conditions before and after union recognition while Vicky did not.

John Sargent reported that the Little Steel strike of 1937, which most labor historians consider a defeat, was, from his point of view, a "victory of great proportions." The steelworkers did not win a contract. What they did get was an agreement through the governor's office that the company would recognize and bargain with "the Steelworkers Union and the company union and any other organization that wanted to represent the people in the steel industry."

Without a contract, without any agreement with the company, without any regulations concerning hours of work, conditions of work, or wages, a tremendous surge took place. We talk of a rank-and-file movement: the beginning of union organization was the best kind of rank-and-file movement you could think of. John L. Lewis sent in a few organizers, but there were no organizers at Inland Steel. . . . The union organizers were essentially workers in the mill who were so disgusted with their conditions and so ready for a change that they took the union into their own hands.

Without a contract, John continued,

we secured for ourselves agreements on working conditions and wages that we do not have today [1970]. For example, as a result of the enthusiasm of the people in the mill you had a series of strikes, wildcats, shut-downs, slow-downs, anything working people could think of to secure for themselves what they decided they had to have. If their wages were low there was no contract to prohibit them from striking, and they struck for better wages. If their conditions were bad, if they didn't like what was going on, if they were being abused, the people in the mill themselves—without a contract or any agreement with the company involved—would shut down a department or even a group of departments to secure for themselves the things they found necessary.

Sargent went on to say that in the late 1930s, Local 1010 made an agreement with Inland Steel that the company would not pay less than any of its competitors throughout the country. All that a union representative had to do was to prove to the company that a particular category of workers, for example on the pickle line, was being paid less than similar steelworkers at, say, Youngstown Sheet & Tube in Youngstown. "And if that was a fact, we were given an increase of wages at Inland."[5]

Nick Migas, who was a grievance committeeman in the Inland Steel open hearth, offered further particulars. "We organized departmental meetings," he remembered. "Every month the department would meet at the union hall, and discuss their immediate problems, work things out, and decide what to do about it." In later years, a

---

5. Patterson, Reese, and Sargent, "Your Dog Don't Bark No More," in *Rank and File*, ed. Lynd and Lynd (expanded edition), pp. 107–8.

worker would file a grievance, the steward would take it up, and that was the last the worker heard about it. But in those early days, "the man who had the grievance came right along with me. . . . He went with me to the next step. . . . He was always there, he knew exactly what his case was, he knew exactly what position the company was taking."

Migas recalled an incident when the company wouldn't settle a grievance for the charging car operators. Management had increased the tonnage without increasing the rate. "So that night it started to slow down, and by the next morning there were two furnaces where they had to shut the heat off. They settled the grievance in a hurry. Nobody told anybody to strike. There was just that close relationship, working with the people, where they knew what was necessary."[6]

Clearly what John Sargent and Nick Migas felt they learned at Inland Steel was very similar to the analysis projected a generation earlier by the IWW.[7] A comprehensive collective bargaining agreement, assumed by today's labor historians and union organizers to be self-evidently desirable, was for these men an obstacle. At Inland Steel, local union officers were empowered by the 1937 strike settlement that obligated the company to bargain with their members-only union. They felt that they were in a stronger position before the union was "recognized" as exclusive bargaining representative than they were afterward. Today's typical contract clauses prohibiting strikes during the life of the agreement, and giving the company the sole right to make investment decisions like shutting down a plant, did not yet exist. The local union could decide for itself into what agreements with the company, if any, it wished to enter.

This was a perspective almost unimaginably heretical from the standpoint of today's union leaders and their academic supporters.

Marty Glaberman's Punching Out

Another moment of enlightenment, synthesizing for me the many oral histories Alice and I had conducted, occurred early in the 1970s. A friend handed me a pamphlet titled *Punching Out*. It was the

---

6. Nick Migas, "How the International Took Over," in *Rank and File*, ed. Lynd and Lynd (expanded edition), pp. 163–75.
7. See "Guerrilla History in Gary," based on conversations with "John Smith" (John Sargent) and his colleague "Jim Brown" (Jim Balanoff), in *From Here to There*, pp. 152–58.

product of a small group that called itself Facing Reality and had for the most part been written by a man named Martin Glaberman, known to his friends as "Marty." Later, I became a close friend of Marty's, and edited a collection of his writings.[8]

A one-sentence summary of *Punching Out* is that in a workplace where there is a contract that contains a clause prohibiting strikes for the duration of the agreement (as do almost all collective bargaining agreements in the United States), the shop steward becomes a cop for the boss. The steward must advise workers not to strike, and stand at the plant door warning them of possible consequences as they file into the parking lot on a "wildcat."

At the time he drafted *Punching Out*, Glaberman was working in unionized automobile plants in metropolitan Detroit. One source of the analysis presented in the pamphlet was Marty's poignant personal relationship with a comrade named Johnny Zupan who became a UAW shop steward. "I recruited him [as a member of the Facing Reality group]," Marty recalled, "and I spoke at his funeral." Zupan exemplified the radical who, upon assuming the office of steward, begins to drift away (without fully realizing it) from the fellow workers who elected him because of the steward's obligation to enforce the contract.

After my experience with John Sargent, *Punching Out* turned my ideas about the labor movement upside down. Instead of seeing unions as "good" institutions that had inexplicably taken "bad" positions toward the seating of Mississippi Freedom Democratic Party delegates in Atlantic City, and, until late in the day, toward the Vietnam War, I encountered confirmation of Burnham's concept that unions in a capitalist society function to stabilize the status quo.

About the same time that I read *Punching Out*, I wrote an article on the possibility of radicalism among steelworkers in the early 1930s.[9] I wrote it while still living in Chicago, but drew on interviews in Youngstown as well. A man named Leon Callow who

---

8. Martin Glaberman, *Punching Out & Other Writings*, ed. Staughton Lynd (Chicago: Charles H. Kerr, 2002).
9. "The Possibility of Radicalism in the Early 1930s: The Case of Steel," *Radical America* (November/December 1972), reprinted in Staughton Lynd, *Living Inside Our Hope* (Ithaca: Cornell University Press, 1997), pp. 141–58 (without its footnotes), and (with its footnotes) in *Workers' Struggles, Past and Present: A "Radical America" Reader*, ed. James Green (Philadelphia: Temple University Press, 1983), pp. 190–208.

had been part of the Steel and Metal Workers Industrial Union in Ohio during the Communist Party's "third period" shared his memories. John Barbero, who was working at Youngstown Sheet & Tube's Brier Hill Works, took me to the home of the widow of Clarence Irwin. Irwin had been a leader of the effort to create a rank-and-file movement within the Amalgamated Association of Iron, Steel & Tin Workers before the CIO. Mrs. Irwin lent me a scrapbook about her husband's activity, but preferred not to let me see his diary.

Alice and I also interviewed George Patterson, picket line captain at the Memorial Day Massacre of 1937. George said that in the early 1930s he had organized an independent union at U.S. Steel's South Works in Chicago named the Associated Employees. The Associated Employees had mass support. George said that when it called open-air meetings at Bessemer Park in South Chicago the crowds filled the entire area. But, as I recall his words, because the Associated Employees existed at only one steel mill belonging to a corporation that owned many mills, it had power to do no more than "influence the color of the soap in the washroom." So George and his fellow workers became part of the CIO union in steel, the United Steelworkers of America. The USWA was organized from the top down. Its first officers were staff men from John L. Lewis's United Mine Workers. George knew that the new union into which he was leading his fellow workers would be less democratic than the Associated Employees but felt that he had no other choice.[10]

"The Possibility of Radicalism" pinpointed the same critical problem. The strength of the rank-and-file movement was in local unions. Inland Steel had only one facility and so the local union there, which could shut down Inland's production on its own initiative, had considerable leverage. But most steel companies, like U.S. Steel, were national in scope. Had rank and filers found a way to coordinate their local efforts, they might have created a union more militant, more internally democratic, and more independent politically than the CIO union that ultimately came into being, and would have

---

10. See Lizabeth Cohen, *Making a New Deal: Industrial Workers in Chicago, 1919–1939* (New York: Cambridge University Press, 1990), p. 358, quoted in Staughton Lynd's introduction to *"We Are All Leaders": The Alternative Unionism of the Early 1930s* (Urbana and Chicago: University of Illinois Press, 1996), p. 13.

"insisted on writing the right to strike into any labor-management contract that resulted."[11]

2. *Are There Radical Strategies That Might Still Be Explored?*

The Writers' Workshop in Gary not only conducted oral history interviews but also produced pamphlets. At that time, the major steel companies joined together in bargaining with the national Steelworkers union for a single nationwide contract, known as the Basic Steel Contract; 1971 was a year in which steel companies and the national union would bargain for such an agreement. Local unions of steelworkers in northern Indiana and South Chicago were also holding elections that year. Typically candidates would put out platforms that combined limited but popular demands (such as "Give us back our Cost of Living clause") with a more visionary plank, insisting, for example, that "No steelmaking facility should be partly or wholly shut down without union and community input."

With characteristic chutzpah, the Writers' Workshop decided to prepare an imaginary contract that contained only the more visionary demands. At the suggestion of John Sargent's colleague, Jim Balanoff, I sent it to a group unknown to us, the Rank And File Team (RAFT) of Youngstown, Ohio.

As the Lynds were sitting at supper a few nights later, the phone rang. A mighty voice bellowed into the receiver, "Hello. This is Bill Litch from Youngstown. What mill do you work in?" (Bill's voice, we later learned, was unnaturally loud because he had been partially deafened in the mill.) I explained that I was a mere historian. "That's all right," the big voice responded. "We liked your pamphlet."

Litch explained that a few days hence the Rank And File Team would be picketing outside a fancy hotel in Washington, DC, where company and national union negotiators would be holding their initial bargaining, or "sound off," session. I said that, by complete coincidence, I would be in Washington that day. We agreed that I would come to the hotel and join the picket line.

I did so, and after a respectable period of picketing, we adjourned to a nearby coffee shop to get to know each other. Two

11. Staughton Lynd, *Living Inside Our Hope*, pp. 156–57.

of the small group identified themselves as Ed Mann and John Barbero. Both had been Marines in World War II. During the war, John had learned some Japanese as a guard at a prisoner of war camp, and after VJ Day married a young Japanese woman whom he brought back to Youngstown. Ed and John worked at the Brier Hill mill of Youngstown Sheet & Tube. They had both been active in the United Labor Party, a surprising fusion of Trotskyists and members of the IWW with a base in the Akron tire plants. It became clear that they believed in racial equality both in the mill and in the Youngstown community, where swimming pools were still segregated after World War II. They were also civil libertarians, socialists with a small "s," and opponents of both the Korean and Vietnam wars. As we talked, I had the feeling that I would probably never again meet two such workers. Over the next five years, we visited back and forth between Ohio and Illinois. In 1973, Ed Mann became president and John Barbero vice president of Local 1462, United Steelworkers of America, at Brier Hill. Thus they were strategically situated to respond to the closing of Youngstown's major steel mills and the resulting termination of ten thousand basic steel workers.

Meantime, I graduated from the University of Chicago Law School and Alice became a paralegal. With the help of a recommendation from Ed Mann, we got jobs at Youngstown's leading labor law firm. At the end of July 1976, we moved to an industrial suburb seven miles north of Youngstown called Niles.

In Youngstown, the closing of a major steel mill was announced in each of three successive years: 1977, 1978, and 1979. By the summer of 1980, no steel was being made in the city.

With each shutdown announcement, the community's understanding deepened. When the closing of the Campbell Works was announced in September 1977, popular sentiment blamed the federal government for imposing unreasonable environmental standards and for letting foreign steel into the country. The announcement in 1978 that Brier Hill would be shut down caused local public opinion to target the Lykes steamship company that had acquired Youngstown Sheet & Tube and, so it was said, used the steel company as a "cash cow" for additional acquisitions. The final closings, announced by U.S. Steel in November 1979, resulted in direct action inspired by Ed Mann, and litigation in which I served as lead counsel.

The Shutdown Saga: Ed's Story

Ed says that, like most area steelworkers, he had assumed the mill would always be there.[12] In October 1978, steelworkers at the Brier Hill Works learned otherwise. The first notice to the local union was in a prospectus mailed to stockholders concerning a proposed merger between the Lykes conglomerate, owner of the Youngstown Sheet & Tube steel company, and the Ling Temco Vought (LTV) conglomerate, owner of Jones & Laughlin (J&L) Steel. The prospectus described phasing out Brier Hill as one of the "anticipated benefits" of the merger.

Local 1462 organized a picket line at the mill. About two hundred steelworkers carried signs reading "Keep Brier Hill Open," "People First, Profits Second," "Youngstown, Victim of Corporate Rape," and "Save Our Valley." This was the first direct action taken by steelworkers in response to the Youngstown shutdowns.

On January 22, 1979, Local 1462 held a meeting at the union hall. Ed was chairing the meeting. By coincidence, Gordon Allen, Sheet & Tube's superintendent, was speaking that same evening at the Mahoning Country Club not far away. Ed mentioned that Allen was speaking nearby, and said he still had the signs from the picket line in the back of his truck. People began moving toward the door.

Everyone drove to the Country Club and set up a picket line outside the front door. One guy kept saying, "Let's go inside." Finally, John Barbero led the group into the lobby. Picketers set up a chant: "Where's Gordon Allen?" It was a way of asking whether the workers would ever get to talk to somebody who could make a decision to save the plant.[13]

---

12. What follows is drawn from *We Are the Union: The Story of Ed Mann*, published by the Workers Solidarity Club of Youngstown. It is based on oral histories recorded by Pat Rosenthal, Bruce Nelson, and Staughton and Alice Lynd. Excerpts from the text of *We Are the Union* are reproduced in *Rank and File*, ed. Lynd and Lynd (expanded edition), pp. 362–63. Ed Mann and John Barbero speak often and vividly in *Shout Youngstown*, a documentary film by Youngstown natives Dorie Krauss and Carol Greenwald Brouder about the closings of Youngstown's steel mills. *Shout Youngstown* can be obtained from Cinema Guild, Inc., 115 W. 30th St., Suite 800, New York, NY 10001; 800-723-5522; www.cinemaguild.com.
13. *The Brier Hill Unionist*, vol. 6, no. 4 (February 1979), published a photo of members of Local 1462 with their picket signs inside the Mahoning Country Club confronting Gordon Allen. The video *Shout Youngstown* includes narration of the encounter by eye witnesses Gerald Dickey, Local 1462 Recording Secretary, and me.

The management of the Country Club called the police. However, the police made no attempt to interfere.

J&L's Youngstown district manager and superintendent of industrial relations pleaded with Ed to keep the demonstrators outside. After a heated discussion, they agreed to hold people in the lobby until Allen came out. The people waited ten or fifteen minutes.

When Allen finally came out, he paused, looked up, and said, "Now Ed, you know we are handling this through the union." Ed and several others responded in one voice, "We *are* the union!"

In November 1979, U.S. Steel announced that it was closing all its mills in the Youngstown area. Another 3,500 workers would lose their jobs. Later that month, about three hundred Youngstown steelworkers, together with Pittsburgh supporters, occupied the first two floors of U.S. Steel's national headquarters in Pittsburgh for several hours.

On January 28, 1980, there was a rally at the Steelworkers' Local 1330 hall just up the hill from U.S. Steel's Youngstown administration building. Politicians came and made speeches. Then Ed spoke.

He began by saying, "You know, we've heard a lot about benefits this morning, but I thought we were here to save jobs." Then he went on:

> I think we've got a job to do today. And that job is to let U.S. Steel know that this is the end of the line. No more jobs are going to be shut down in Youngstown. You've got men here, you've got women here, you've got children here and we're here for one purpose. Not to be talked to about what's going to happen in Congress two years from now. What's going to happen in Youngstown today?
>
> There's a building two blocks from here. That's the U.S. Steel headquarters. You know the whole country is looking at the voters, the citizens. What are you going to do? Are you going to make an action, or are you going to sit and be talked to?
>
> The action is today. We're going down that hill, and we're going to let the politicians know, we're going to let U.S. Steel know, we're going to let the whole country know that steelworkers in Youngstown got guts and we want to fight for our jobs. We're not going to fight for welfare! [Cheers.]

In 1919, the fight was on for the eight-hour day and they lost that struggle and they burned down East Youngstown, which is Campbell. Now I'm not saying burn anything down but you got the eight-hour day.

In 1937, you wanted a union and people got shot in Youngstown because they wanted a union. And everything hasn't been that great since you got a union. Every day, you put your life on the line when you went into that iron house. Every day, you sucked up the dirt and took a chance on breaking your legs or breaking your back. And anyone who's worked in there knows what I'm talking about.

At that point, this white working-class radical in Youngstown, Ohio, did a remarkable thing. He read to the impatient crowd a long passage by a nineteenth-century African American.

Now, I don't like to read to people, but in 1857 Frederick Douglass said something that I think you ought to listen to:

"Those who profess to favor freedom and yet discourage agitation are men who want crops without plowing up the ground. They want rain without thunder and lightning. They want the ocean without the awful roar of its waters. This struggle may be a moral one [and you've heard a lot about that] or it may be a physical one [and you're going to hear about that] but it must be a struggle. Power concedes nothing without a demand. It never did and it never will. Find out what people will submit to and you will find out the exact measure of injustice and wrong which will be imposed upon them. And these will be continued until they are resisted in either words or blows or with both. The limits of tyrants are prescribed by the endurance of those they oppress."

This was said in 1857 and things haven't changed. U.S. Steel is going to see how much they can put on you. And when I say you, I mean Youngstown, you know. We've got lists. We've got an obituary of plants that were shut down in the last twenty years. When are we going to make a stand?

Ed Mann then concluded: "Now, I'm going down that hill and I'm going into that building. And anyone that doesn't want to come along doesn't have to, but I'm sure there are those who'll want to." Plant protection people stepped aside and at least seven hundred people took over the building.

At the end of the afternoon, Bob Vasquez, president of Local 1330, decided to end the occupation. But, Ed concluded, "If we had it to do again, I know that he, and I, and everyone I know who was there, would have stayed in that building for as long as it took."

The struggle to reopen the mills convinced me more than ever that only outright public ownership, if need be without compensation, could adequately respond to the flight of manufacturing production and investment.

I came away from the struggle with another conviction as well: that only local unions, not any national union or federation of national unions, could be looked to for visionary energy and seeds of change. Both in Youngstown and Pittsburgh local unions, not the United Steelworkers of America, were central to the effort in alliance with local churches and individual clergy. In Youngstown, two local union officers (Gerald Dickey and Duane Irving) left their positions to become for a period full-time organizers for the Ecumenical Coalition of the Mahoning Valley, a coalition of local churches. Six local unions became plaintiffs in a lawsuit that sought to reopen Ohio mills. Similarly in the Monongahela Valley of Pennsylvania, grievance chairpersons at the gigantic Homestead Works and railroad equipment manufacturer Union Switch and Signal (Mike Stout and Charlie McCollester) led the effort to stop the shutdowns. The national Steelworkers union stood aside from or actually sabotaged these efforts.

The Workers Solidarity Club

Soon after the mills closed, a local union made up of workers for the local electric utility company asked me to lead a class on filing grievances and NLRB charges. The following year, I was asked to teach another class on any subject of my choosing. By that time, I had come to believe that many rank-and-file workers in the Youngstown area, a hotbed of union sentiment in the 1930s, were deeply disillusioned by the current state of the labor movement. I said that I thought we should share our experiences and try to figure out what had gone wrong.

At the end of the class, the participants wanted to go on meeting. Utility Workers 118 had recently been on strike, had appealed for help to the Mahoning County central labor union, and had been disappointed by the response. The idea emerged that our group, if it continued, could be a "parallel central labor union" that assisted area workers who were on strike, with firewood, publicity, and warm bodies for the picket line. After some discussion, my wife suggested the name "Workers Solidarity Club of Youngstown."

A crucial aspect of the Club was that from the very first meeting most of those in the room were workers. Too often, Left intellectuals gather together and ask each other, "Now, how can we attract workers?" When workers show up, they are a minority. The culture and vocabulary of the meetings have already been established by middle-class conveners, and the workers soon leave.

It was also critical, in my perception, that from the beginning there were many different kinds of workers in the circle. (We always met in a circle.) Unlike other radical groups we felt no need to "raise consciousness" by preaching class solidarity. As a steelworker, a discharged shop steward from the local bakery, a nurse, a truck driver, or an SEIU organizer who wanted to form a union of fellow organizers, listened to each other's tales of woe, a sense of class came about naturally. At the end of each meeting we stood, held hands, and sang the first and last verses of "Solidarity Forever."

For the next fifteen years, workers in the area knew that on the second Wednesday of each month there was a place where they could go for help.

The Workers Solidarity Club had no officers. If someone had invited a guest, or was concerned about a particular problem, that someone was likely to lead the discussion for the evening. As in Stan Weir's description of the "informal work group," however, Ed Mann exercised an unspoken moral authority.[14] He had "gone down that hill" and led the occupation of U.S. Steel's administrative headquarters to protest the closing of U.S. Steel's facilities in the Valley. He had walked his talk.

One other practice of the Workers Solidarity Club served us well. We felt no need to approve an activity as an organization before individual members of the Club ventured forth to undertake it. Instead, Ed or I or anyone would say something like, "Driving over here, I saw that the So-and-So workers had a picket line. I stopped

---

14. See Stan Weir, "The Informal Work Group," in *Rank and File*, ed. Lynd and Lynd (expanded edition), pp.177–200.

and asked them if they needed help. I'm going back tomorrow morning with a load of firewood. Anyone want to come with me?" It was leading by example. And it worked.

Two memorable actions of the Workers Solidarity Club illustrate the possibilities of a qualitatively different kind of unionism.

Trumbull Memorial Hospital

On July 31, 1982, the 717 service and maintenance workers at Trumbull Memorial Hospital in Warren, Ohio (near Youngstown) went on strike.[15]

Most of the strikers were women, and even though they were members of an AFSCME local union their wages were lower than the wages of workers at non-union hospitals in the area.

The hospital began to hire strikebreakers, or "scabs," early in the strike. The local union had not prepared for this contingency. Scabs were permitted to report for work without resistance.

After the hospital began to hire scabs, one union officer is alleged to have told the membership they might as well give up. They refused.

Two members of the Workers Solidarity Club went to the picket line to ask the women what help they needed. Then members of the Club met in the Lynds' basement to discuss what was to be done. Alice Lynd took notes. At the end of the evening, it was agreed that the Club should prepare and distribute a leaflet. Alice read her notes aloud, and they became the basis for the Club's first leaflet. It began, "THINK before you cross a picket line. Think before you take your neighbor's job." The leaflet ended, "WE WILL BE PICKETING AT TRUMBULL MEMORIAL HOSPITAL EVERY WEDNESDAY AT 5 P.M. IN SUPPORT OF THE STRIKE. JOIN US."

The word about the Wednesday afternoon rallies spread informally. The rallies became larger and larger, and started earlier. Members of other unions came with banners and homemade signs. The crowd chanted slogans like "Warren is a union town. We won't let you tear it down."

---

15. The account that follows is based on a Workers Solidarity Club pamphlet titled *The Trumbull Memorial Hospital Strike* written by "Jane Shapira and Staughton Lynd, with the assistance of many others, quoted and unquoted," and published by Inkwell Press, a worker-owned cooperative.

On October 2, a throng of union supporters marched from downtown Warren to the hospital. A participant remembered:

> There were marchers from sidewalk to sidewalk. There were police at every intersection along the route. The police were friendly. There were also families with little children, sitting on the grass or in cars, and people in front of stores. There was a sense that everybody cared, even if they couldn't take part in it.

Early in the strike, Judge David Griffiths of the Trumbull County Court of Common Pleas issued an injunction, limiting picketing to four persons at each hospital entrance. Ed Mann was charged with contempt of the injunction.

The hearing on the contempt charge took place in a courtroom crowded with strikers who filled every seat and stood against the courtroom walls. Ed was called to the stand. The judge asked him why he had disobeyed the injunction. Ed answered, "What injunction?" A conviction for acting in contempt of a court injunction requires proof that the injunction has been "served," which in labor disputes generally means, read aloud in the presence of the defendant. The State was unable to prove that Ed Mann had been served. The judge took a long moment to survey the large number of potential voters in the room and said, in effect, "Well, now you know about the injunction, so don't do it again." Wednesday afternoon rallies continued and grew even bigger.

Emboldened, the crowd at the Wednesday afternoon rally on October 13 decided to go to the homes of hospital trustees who lived nearby on a street named, unbelievably, Country Club Lane. The trustees were management people. There was no African-American trustee, and the only woman was in a management position. As one striker recalled her feelings, "The Board of Trustees was made up of people who have something. They don't represent the community."

The crowd approached one home on Country Club Lane. Jean Maurice, a member of another AFSCME local union, and Tony Budak, who worked at a nearby factory, attempted to deliver a petition. When the door was not opened, Ms. Maurice wrote on the front door with her lipstick. Police officers arrived, arrested Ms. Maurice, and placed her in a police car. Just as at Sproul Plaza in Berkeley in the fall of 1964, protesters sat down around the police car so that it could not move. Bill Malone, officer of another local union, went up to one of the officers to talk to him. He was pushed to the ground, roughed up, handcuffed, and arrested.

Finally, Ms. Maurice was removed by the police, and the crowd drifted back to the hospital. The Warren police ordered the crowd to disperse. The demonstrators moved slowly backward, off the street and on to the sidewalk.

The line of police converged on Mr. Mann. A striker's wife says that the police "passed by a good number of people, including myself and my family, to get Ed." Mann was placed under arrest, dragged across the street by local police officers, and charged with aggravated riot and resisting arrest. It took years before the Ohio Supreme Court found his arrest to have been unlawful.

The intervention of the Workers Solidarity Club saved the local union. The NLRB found the hospital guilty of a variety of unfair labor practices. One of these ULPs was increasing its bargaining demands after the union had accepted the employer's bargaining offer. On December 17, 1982, strikers voted 194–52 to ratify a contract that included a 19.5 percent wage increase spread over the three-year life of the contract, and a timetable for recall of strikers over a twenty-month period.

The Workers Solidarity Club concluded that the main lesson of the Trumbull Memorial Strike was that rank-and-file workers must develop their own strength, and depend on themselves. When as at TMH the rank and file are mostly women, and their leaders are all men, this is especially true. The women who kept the strike going needed times and places where they could exchange feelings and ideas, and make their own decisions. This didn't happen at union meetings. It happened at little gatherings at the union hall when the women cooked soup, played cards, distributed food, and "tried to keep themselves together."

Jean Maurice sums up this way: "I lost a lot by being involved at TMH. . . . But I gained more than I lost. I've grown as a person, in strength, confidence, and conviction. I'm less afraid—although not yet completely unafraid—to stand up for what I believe in."

The Buick Youngstown "Honkathon"

Several years later another local union, a Machinists Union local, went on strike against a local car dealer. Once again, help from the sponsoring national and state union organizations was negligible.

Once again, the local court issued an injunction. In this case, the judge tried to find a striker in contempt who had brought coffee to the two men that the injunction permitted to picket at a certain entrance to the workplace.

In response, supporting trade unionists generated what came to be called a "beepathon" or "honkathon." The injunction limited the number of persons who could be stationed at a given entrance. Accordingly, a wide array of union members would assemble at a time of the week when the dealership was especially busy (like Saturday afternoon), and drive a procession of cars very slowly down the main street adjacent to the employer's premises, with provocative signs displayed, and horns blaring.

We were not violating an injunction about the number of persons who could be stationed at a particular place. We were exercising our right as citizens to drive along a busy city thoroughfare. Bill DePietro, president of the embattled local union, remembered the first Honkathon this way:

> There were seventy-five cars, driving real slow. It went all the way from the school, up the back, and around. The cops were so tickled that we weren't marching that they held up traffic for us, remember? We went back and forth. People were in their cars, holding up signs, driving one after the other. The signs said "Scabs," "Sweeney [who managed the dealership] is a union buster." We honked and honked. I burned out two of my horns. But it was well worth it.

After that, DePietro continued, "we did it two nights a week. It was good for morale. You didn't need too many cars." And it "drove the company nuts."[16]

Management settled and, as in the Trumbull Memorial Hospital struggle, the local union survived.

Solidarity Unionism

In May 1990 a conference was held in Minneapolis on "Workers' Self-Organization." My friend Stan Weir had been invited to give

---

16. Bill DiPietro, "They're Not Scabs Any More," in *Rank and File*, ed. Lynd and Lynd (expanded edition), p. 343.

the keynote address, but Stan became ill, and I was invited to take his place.

I found myself on the upper floor of an old, cavernous building that must have housed dozens of similar gatherings over the years. I had resolved to try to pull together what I felt I had learned as a labor historian and labor lawyer over the previous twenty years. I "let it all hang out," talking on and on as the delegates no doubt became more and more hungry for lunch. Afterward, David Roediger suggested that I publish the talk as a booklet. He had connections with the publisher Charles H. Kerr and the book appeared in 1992 under the title *Solidarity Unionism: Rebuilding the Labor Movement from Below.*

A big chunk of the 1990 talk that became the booklet, *Solidarity Unionism*, had to do with labor history. If we were disappointed by the results of CIO and AFL-CIO unionism, we needed to be as clear as possible about what really happened and what might have been done differently.

As I and others have dug into memories and documentary records of the 1930s, one important discovery has been that many groups such as the IWW, the Communist Party, and the American Civil Liberties Union (ACLU), and many individuals such as A.J. Muste, Roger Baldwin of the ACLU, and my father Robert Lynd, during at least some periods, opposed, or expressed grave reservations about, the National Labor Relations Act of 1935.

The ACLU's misgivings sprang from "deep involvement in a bitter jurisdictional dispute between two rival unions in the bituminous coalfields of southern Illinois." The ACLU had been concerned throughout the 1920s about the dictatorial style of John L. Lewis, president of the United Mine Workers (UMW). In late 1932, dissident miners had bolted District 12 of the UMW to form the Progressive Miners of America. When the National Industrial Recovery Act (NIRA) was enacted in June 1933, Baldwin feared

> that Lewis would succeed in having included in the bituminous coal code labor provisions giving the UMW exclusive bargaining rights, employer checkoff of union dues, and a closed shop. Baldwin was convinced that such a development would surely threaten the destruction of the Progressive Miners and, thereby, deny the right of thousands

of miners in Illinois to be represented by a union of their own choosing.[17]

Recent research by Professor James Pope of Rutgers University Law School suggests that Baldwin's apprehensions about John L. Lewis were well founded. Pope writes that "according to the standard story" of labor history in the 1930s, in May 1933 Lewis, anticipating the enactment of section 7(a) of the National Industrial Recovery Act, committed the entire treasury of the United Mine Workers to a massive organizing campaign in the soft coalfields. Thanks to Lewis's far-sighted leadership, we have been told, in little more than a year UMW membership quintupled, from about a hundred thousand to about half a million.

The reality, according to Pope, was altogether different. Miners in southwestern Pennsylvania began to organize more than two and a half months before the passage of the NIRA. Paid UMW staff initially opposed the rank-and-file initiatives or dragged their feet. Pope says that Lewis was

> a step behind the local union activists. His celebrated organizing campaign was not launched until after rank-and-file miners had already rejuvenated the union. Once deployed, his organizers worked persistently to undermine the strike movement that eventually delivered the code. . . . Thus, the sensational recovery of the UMW—later touted by Lewis as a product of centralized discipline and federal government lawmaking—was in fact brought about by a democratic movement of local activists enforcing their own vision of the right to organize.[18]

The proposed National Labor Relations Act (NLRA) or Wagner Act did not allay Roger Baldwin's concerns. He wrote to Senator Wagner that no federal agency such as the proposed National Labor Relations Board

---

17. Cletus E. Daniel, *The ACLU and the Wagner Act: An Inquiry into the Depression-Era Crisis of American Liberalism* (Ithaca: New York State School of Industrial and Labor Relations, Cornell University, 1980), pp. 33–34.
18. James Gray Pope, "The Western Pennsylvania Coal Strike of 1933, Part I: Lawmaking from Below and the Revival of the United Mine Workers," *Labor History*, vol. 44, no. 1 (2003), pp. 15–48.

intervening in the conflicts between employers and employees can be expected fairly to determine the issues of labor's rights. We say this from a long experience with the various boards set up in Washington, all of which have tended to take from labor its basic right to strike by substituting mediation, conciliation, or, in some cases, arbitration.[19]

In fact, Senator Wagner and his principal draftsman, Leon Keyserling, were only too well aware that their law might be used to try to take away the strike weapon. Section 13 of the law as enacted explicitly guarantees the right to strike. Asked whether there was some specific reason for this language, Keyserling answered:

> There was a definite reason. . . . [Senator] Wagner was always strong for the right to strike on the ground that without the right to strike, which was labor's ultimate weapon, they really had no other weapon. That guarantee . . . was particularly necessary because a lot of people made the argument that because the government was giving labor the right to bargain collectively, that was a substitute for the right to strike, which was utterly wrong.[20]

One other critical historical issue should be briefly mentioned. The seniority system is commonly regarded as the signature achievement of the CIO's "workplace contractualism." Labor historians David Montgomery and Ronald Schatz tell us, "Before the 1930s the seniority principle was seldom found in union rules or contracts, as they applied to layoffs. . . . [With the industrial unions of the 1930s] the seniority rule became so basic a part of American life that many workers today find it difficult to imagine any other principle as just."[21] But while the reason for seniority in hiring and promotion is obvious, its use in layoffs is more questionable. In the typical workplace, strict application of seniority to layoffs may cause recently hired minorities

---

19. Daniel, *The ACLU and the Wagner Act*, p. 101.

20. Kenneth M. Casebeer, "Holder of the Pen: An Interview with Leon Keyserling on Drafting the Wagner Act," *University of Miami Law Review*, vol. 42, no. 2 (November 1987), p. 353.

21. David Montgomery and Ronald Schatz, "Facing Layoffs," *Radical America*, vol. 10, no. 2 (March/April 1976), pp. 18–19.

and women to be put on the street with nothing while elderly white males continue to work overtime.

Many workers have understood this, and found ways to circumvent the use of seniority in layoffs so as to distribute work evenly. There is strong evidence that independent local unions prior to the formation of the CIO, and local unions of a national union like the United Electrical Workers, considered that dividing work equally among what Stan Weir called the "family at work" was an essential means of building solidarity.[22] The Legal Services office where I was working when President Reagan cut our budget 20 percent did exactly the same thing. All the lawyers "went down" to a four-day work week, regardless of when they had been hired.

Conclusion

Later events reinforced my belief in what I had learned in Chicago and Youngstown. Over the years, labor activists of all political persuasions repeatedly placed their faith in a new top leader for the trade union movement only to be disappointed, whether that leader was named Arnold Miller, Ed Sadlowski, Ron Carey, John Sweeney, Andrew Stern, or Richard Trumka. In 1995, John Sweeney, president of the Service Employees International Union, became president of the AFL-CIO. A long list of intellectuals signed a public letter, drafted by two labor historians, praising Sweeney's election as the most important political event since the civil rights movement of the 1960s and pledging their support for his supposed "democratic" aspirations. But I knew from interviewing a rank-and-file hospital worker named Andrea Carney that, just before becoming AFL-CIO president, Sweeney had put into trusteeship SEIU Local 399

---

22. The Progressive Miners championed by Roger Baldwin opposed John L. Lewis's support for mechanization, and proposed the alternative of "job sharing or equalization of work" as a means of controlling the mechanization of the workplace and keeping operating mines in production. Carl D. Oblinger, *Divided Kingdom: Work, Community, and the Mining Wars in the Central Illinois Coal Fields During the Great Depression* (Springfield: Illinois State Historical Society, 2004), pp. 20–21. A dramatic example of a local union of the United Electrical Workers dividing available work equally among everyone in the workplace is described by Mia Giunta in *Rank and File*, ed. Lynd and Lynd (expanded edition), pp. 322–34. This happened in the 1970s.

at Kaiser Permanente in Los Angeles after a "multiracial alliance" had elected a new local union executive board.[23]

The transition from the "organizing" strategy that I deplore to the "accompanying" approach that I advocate has been memorably described by Stan Weir. Stan reports that in the 1950s "[t]he McCarthy period had disintegrated my political group considerably." When he was hired by a General Motors plant in the San Francisco area, "there was no movement telling me what to do. I was 'just a worker.'"[24]

He continues: "A whole new world opened up to me. I began to see that to approach any situation like this with a whole set of preconceived slogans was way off the beam." Stan came to feel that he was part of an informal work group, a "family at work," with a distinctive subculture that he had to learn. He made friends with the people around him in the usual way. They were working night shift and the practice developed that when they came off work they would go to the home of a member of the group to eat and talk. "And the politics I injected into the group? . . . Just being *me* was being political."

Similarly Bill DiPietro, president of the local union at the Buick car dealership in Youngstown, has the following to say about "organizing":

> The international unions want to do good, but they don't know how to organize. You can't organize the way they want to do it.
>
> The Machinists international had a class in Berkeley. They brought people in and said, "Here's how we figure we're going to organize." I gave them a good listen. I want to organize, too.
>
> Then I went up to the man who made the presentation and said, "It's never going to happen." He says, "Why?" I says, "Because you're not going to bring maybe ten guys in, and zoom into this town, like maybe Youngstown, and say, 'OK, we're going to organize this. We're going to talk to people about why they should be in the union.'" Those are

23. Andrea Carney, "I Declined to Join the Staff," in *Rank and File*, ed. Lynd and Lynd (expanded edition), pp. 386–87.
24. Stan Weir, "The Informal Work Group," in *Rank and File* (expanded edition), pp. 196–97.

great words. But if you're not going to be there every day, you can't do it. People will tell them, "I don't want to talk to you. I want to see what you can do."[25]

I agree with Bill, and also with Ed Mann when he said:

A lot of our folks belong to established unions and they don't want to attack the AFL-CIO because they feel that by doing that you're attacking the union movement. I don't sense that there's any movement there at all. We have people who are sensitive about attacking the AFL-CIO for not doing its job. But it's not going to do its job. It's not structured to do its job.[26]

"I don't regard the AFL-CIO as 'the union,'" Ed went on. "I think the union's in the people."

Ed also emphasized that there is no way to predict when collective insurgency will become possible, and so the task of the organizer is to accompany, and thus to be present, to be available.

It's very unpredictable. If we read our history, we know that back in Debs' time the railroads were one of the biggest industries in the country. They had a lot of shops: people worked as blacksmiths, machinists, whatever. The company cut their pay so much a day. They didn't do anything about it. Six months later the company cut their pay again, quite a bit. Then the company came up with a pay cut that was infinitesimal. That was enough! The whole country went down. It was like a general strike. They burned the railroad yards in Pittsburgh and in many other places. Who knows what is going to make the workers say, This is enough! But the point is, somebody has to be there when they say, This is enough![27]

---

25. Bill DiPietro, "They're Not Scabs Any More," in *Rank and File* (expanded edition), p. 345.
26. Ed Mann, "I'm Going Down That Hill," in *Rank and File* (expanded edition), p. 365.
27. Ibid.

Finally, I agree with Ed when he stressed that we need a new kind of labor movement, something qualitatively different. "Maybe the CIO has run its course," Ed concluded. "Maybe there will be unions but they won't be structured as we see them today."

For Ed, and for me, the IWW comes closer to the kind of labor movement that we need than any of the larger and more obvious alternatives. That doesn't necessarily mean that the IWW will succeed in reinventing itself sufficiently to become a vehicle for masses of people. But that may happen, and in the meantime the IWW provides a model for a movement that is horizontal rather than vertical; that is committed to preserving the possibility of strike action; and that welcomes the never-ending creation of new local institutions from below. Above all, the IWW stands for a society committed to mutual aid and solidarity. As Ed put it,

> The Wobblies say, Do away with the wage system. For a lot of people that's pretty hard to take. What the Wobblies mean is, you'll have what you need. The wage system has destroyed us. If I work hard I'll get ahead, but if I'm stronger than Jim over here, maybe I'll get the better job and Jim will be sweeping floors. But maybe Jim has four kids. The wage system is a very divisive thing. It's the only thing we have now, but it's very divisive.

"Maybe I'm just dreaming," Ed Mann said, "but I think there's a better way."[28]

---

28. Ibid.

The Civil Rights Movement

THE RELATIONSHIP BETWEEN STAFF WORKERS OF THE STUDENT Nonviolent Coordinating Committee (SNCC), and African Americans in the Deep South who sought the right to vote was, while it lasted, beyond question a relationship of organizing in the spirit of accompaniment. Perhaps the most evocative descriptions are by Charles Payne, writing about SNCC's work in Greenwood, Mississippi, and Barbara Ransby, in her biography of SNCC mentor Ella Baker.

Because the concept of "accompaniment" appears to have originated in El Salvador, is associated with Latin American liberation theology, and is expounded by aid workers in the less-developed world such as Dr. Paul Farmer, the idea is commonly regarded as an import into the United States. Charles Payne, however, insists that some activists "working in the South prior to the 1960s left . . . a distinct philosophical heritage" with a fundamental emphasis on "the ability of the oppressed to participate in the shaping of their own lives."[1] Preeminent among these were Septima Clark, Ella Baker, and Myles Horton. "All three espoused a non-bureaucratic style of work, focused on local problems, sensitive to the social structure of local communities, appreciative of the culture of those communities." The important thing was

> the development of efficacy in those most affected by a problem. Over the long run, whether a community achieved this or that tactical objective was likely to matter less than whether the people in it came to see themselves as having the right and the capacity to have some say-so in their own lives.

Getting people to feel that way, Payne continues,

> requires participatory political and educational activities, in which the people themselves have a part in defining the

---

1. Charles M. Payne, *I've Got the Light of Freedom: The Organizing Tradition and the Mississippi Freedom Struggle* (Berkeley: University of California Press, 1995), pp. 67–68.

problems—"Start where the people are"—and solving them. Not even organizations founded in the name of the poor can be relied upon. In the end, people have to learn to rely on themselves.[2]

Of the three persons designated by Charles Payne as creators of this philosophical heritage, he and Barbara Ransby agree that the most influential was Ella Baker. For "Ms. Baker" (as she was always referred to),

> the model of the Good Life was not derived from the lifestyle of middle-class whites, as it was for some of her NAACP colleagues, nor from any pre-cut ideological scheme, as it was for some of her Marxist acquaintances. During the decades when Blacks were fleeing the South, physically and often emotionally, she was trying to recreate the spirit of the self-sufficient, egalitarian people who raised her.[3]

Ms. Baker said of the trade union movement that emerged by the end of the 1930s, "I'm afraid it succumbed, to a large extent to what I call the American weakness of being recognized and taking on the characteristics and values even of the foe."[4]

After the Montgomery, Alabama bus boycott in 1955, Ms. Baker joined the staff of the Southern Christian Leadership Conference (SCLC), headed by Martin Luther King, Jr. But there was constant tension between herself and the black male ministers who composed SCLC. They practiced a top-down style of leadership. She thought that a sensible structure for bringing about social change "would have small groups of people . . . retaining contact in some form with other such cells."

The Student Nonviolent Coordinating Committee (SNCC) was created at a conference that Ms. Baker organized with $800 from SCLC. At the founding conference, just such small groups of people as Ms. Baker imagined, who had launched sit-ins in different parts of the South, came together.

---

2. Ibid., p. 68.
3. Ibid., p. 81.
4. Ibid., p. 83.

Barbara Ransby, in her book-long appreciation of Ms. Baker, identifies similarities between Ella Baker and radical ideologues in other countries. She calls Ms. Baker "a Freirian teacher [and] a Gramscian intellectual."[5] Like Italian Communist Antonio Gramsci, Ella Baker felt that the radical intellectual should not simply write books and give speeches but become an "organic intellectual," accompanying ordinary people in their day-to-day struggles. Like the Brazilian educator Paulo Freire, she called attention to how much poor people already know and insisted that part of teaching "was the ability to humble oneself and simply listen." Ms. Baker "emphasized the importance of tapping oppressed communities for their own knowledge." She affirmed in her practice and her teachings "a style of personal grassroots organizing . . . more common among women than men."[6]

Layers of Accompaniment

Accompaniment, as practiced by SNCC in the first half of the 1960s, involved more than the relationship of SNCC staff workers to the African-American communities in which they worked. It also involved the relationship of SNCC staff to one another, and to the volunteers whom they invited to the Deep South.

SNCC field workers experienced countless beatings and incarcerations. In theory they received a periodic pay check from Atlanta headquarters, but in practice they survived by living with poor African-American families. They wore blue jeans on trips to Northern universities as well as in Southern cotton fields. They made decisions by consensus because of a conviction that, as Stokely Carmichael put it, "[n]obody is gonna risk his or her life for a program or policy with which he or she seriously disagrees."[7] Members of SNCC described themselves as "a band of brothers and sisters, standing in a circle of love."

---

5. Barbara Ransby, *Ella Baker & the Black Freedom Movement: A Radical Democratic Vision* (Chapel Hill: University of North Carolina Press, 2003), chapter 12.
6. Ibid., pp. 361 (Gramsci), 362 (listening to what poor people already know), 364 (an organizing style more common among women than men).
7. Stokely Carmichael, *Ready for Revolution: The Life and Struggles of Stokely Carmichael (Kwame Ture)* (New York: Scribner, 2003), p. 300.

In 1964, SNCC staff invited college students to join them in Mississippi for a summer devoted to creation of the Mississippi Freedom Democratic Party (MFDP) and Freedom Schools. In mid-June, volunteers who had been accepted gathered at a college campus near Cincinnati for orientation. The first week was devoted to voter registration and the MFDP. At the end of the first week, that group of volunteers headed for Mississippi and Freedom School volunteers (like myself) arrived. On Sunday, three persons assigned to voter registration—James Chaney, a native Mississippian; Andrew Goodman, a volunteer from New York; and Michael "Mickey" Schwerner, project director in the city of Meridian, Mississippi—disappeared. They had gone to Philadelphia, Mississippi, where a church that was expected to host a Freedom School had been burned to the ground, to look for another site for the school.

At the orientation, there followed hours of frantic telephone calls to the FBI, to Congressmen, and to anxious parents. Rita Schwerner, Mickey's wife, paced the halls, unable to sleep.

Monday evening, everyone came together to hear from Bob Moses of SNCC, principal coordinator of the summer project. Bob spoke very slowly, very softly, often looking down at his shoes. He said that the three missing men had probably been killed. He said that any volunteer who chose to leave at this point would be making an understandable choice, and there would be no criticism. (I was in and out of the meeting, talking with individual Freedom School volunteers struggling with their own feelings and with their parents' apprehensions.)

To the best of my knowledge no one made a tape recording of Bob's remarks. But every one remembers what he said at the end. He said, "For those of you who decide to go on to Mississippi, the only promise I can make is that I will be going with you." I was reminded of a comment by Jack Melancon, a member of the Utopian community in which my wife and I lived for three years in Georgia. Jack said, "Sometimes all you can do for another person is stand in the rain with them." Bob, like Jack, was talking about accompaniment.

Going to Atlantic City

In August 1964, at the end of "Mississippi Freedom Summer," a number of African Americans went to the national Democratic Party convention in Atlantic City, in hope of being seated in place of the all-white delegates of the "regular" Mississippi Democratic Party.

The reason for doing this was because, after three years of intense work, first in southwestern Mississippi and then in the Delta, SNCC had registered very few voters. Not only that: as African Americans emerged from the shadows and demanded their rights as citizens, violence increased also. Most troubling of all, as of early 1964 those who had been killed were not SNCC staff members but courageous local black men such as Herbert Lee (1961), Medgar Evers (1963), and Lewis Allen (1964), not to speak of the many less-well-known black males whose bodies were found floating in a stream or buried in the woods.

The U.S. Department of Justice promised protection to African Americans if they sought to register to vote. But throughout the early 1960s, the federal government consistently failed to provide that protection. Something new was needed, and that something turned out to be the Mississippi Freedom Democratic Party (MFDP).

The MFDP came into being in a step by step, organic manner. And yet, when all is said and done, the MFDP necessarily represented a great deal in which SNCC did *not* believe. It encouraged MFDP members to hope for fundamental change through a national political party that contained racist politicians from across the South. It required MFDP members to take a loyalty oath to President Johnson and the national Democratic Party. Perhaps above all, it transplanted black Mississippians not only outside the geography with which they were familiar, but into a strange new institutional world that caused them to become more dependent on white people, on professional people, and on people from outside their own experience.

It is not entirely clear who first suggested the strategy that evolved into the Freedom Vote of November 1963, the MFDP's trip to Atlantic City in August 1964, and the Congressional Challenge of early 1965. Allard Lowenstein, a peripatetic figure whom the Movement sometimes loved but came to hate, may have drawn on experiences in South Africa to propose this turn to "parallel politics." Longtime SNCC activist and legal adviser Tim Jenkins found an old Mississippi statute that helped in early stages.[8]

---

8. In the ensuing narrative, I follow a forthcoming book by James P. Marshall, the most detailed source known to me on the subject.

Jenkins recalls that he and other law students "discovered an old act which provided that those people who felt that they had been legally denied the right to vote could present themselves on election day, or primary day, at the polling place and sign an affidavit to the effect that they had been illegally denied the right to vote and have their votes counted. . . ." The law had been passed during the time of Reconstruction that followed the Civil War.

Jenkins and his colleagues predicted that twenty thousand African Americans might employ this procedure in a Democratic Party gubernatorial primary to be held on August 6, 1963. The turn-out was much smaller. On reflection, this disappointing showing was recognized to be the result of the hostile atmosphere that prevailed at every registrar's office where a black person might seek to vote. Accordingly, when a runoff in the gubernatorial primary was scheduled for August 27, movement activists proposed a "Vote for Freedom" to be held in more hospitable settings such as African-American churches.

The results of this second "Vote for Freedom" were impressive. African Americans cast more than 27,000 votes, supporting a Mississippi "moderate" named Coleman, 26,721 to 949. Had it been possible for these African-American "freedom votes" to be added to Coleman's total in the official, whites-only primary, Coleman would not have defeated the more racist candidate, Paul Johnson, but he would have considerably reduced Johnson's margin of victory.

When civil rights workers digested this second experience, it seemed clear that (in Lowenstein's words) the Movement had mistakenly limited the candidates "to the ones who were on the Democratic ballot in the runoff. . . . [O]ne had to have a candidate to vote for who stood for what one wanted." What would happen if excluded black Mississippians were given *this* opportunity?

Accordingly, a Freedom Vote was arranged, to be held on the day of the general election in November. Aaron Henry, an African-American pharmacist from Clarksdale and president of the state NAACP, was nominated for governor at a convention in Jackson attended by delegates from SNCC, SCLC, CORE (the Congress of Racial Equality), the NAACP and "various local voters' leagues and civic organizations."[9] Rev. Edwin King, the white chaplain and dean of students at Tougaloo College, was nominated for lieutenant

---

9. Ibid.

governor. Bob Moses became campaign manager. The state executive committee included Charles Evers, who had replaced his murdered brother as State Field Secretary for the NAACP.

"The freedom election was conceived of as a complete rejection of the existing political system," Jenkins remembered. One of the seven objectives of the campaign, as outlined by Dave Dennis of CORE to the organization's national office, was "To encourage Negroes not to support either political party unless they change their civil rights policies."

The final tally in the "Freedom Vote" was over eighty-three thousand, a figure that in the words of James Marshall was "equal to the difference between the [vote totals for the] two official candidates." Over eighty Yale and Stanford students took part in the three-week campaign. Their experiences, together with the media attention they received, suggested the possibility of a "Freedom Summer" in 1964 to which a much larger number of whites from the North would be invited.

The conventional electoral procedures necessary to put the MFDP in position to challenge the "regular" Mississippi delegates for seats at the convention cast a shadow over the process.

To begin with, there was controversy within SNCC as to whether to invite hundreds of white volunteers to Mississippi. Many staff members believed that the presence of so many articulate white college students might discourage African Americans just beginning to engage in citizenly actions such as writing leaflets and speaking in public. So too there was a less well-known controversy within SNCC as to whether the Atlantic City strategy was a good idea.

Going to Atlantic City was different from the Freedom Vote of November 1963. November 1963 was the creation of a symbolic political process for the marginalized and excluded, parallel to the official electoral proceedings. Those who cast "freedom votes" for Henry and King supported candidates other than those on the ballot for the Democratic Party. The purpose was to demonstrate how many African Americans wanted to vote, but were not permitted to do so.

The MFDP in summer 1964, by contrast, expressly sought to assist Mississippi African Americans to become part of the national Democratic Party. And it looked for essential support to Walter Reuther, a trade union leader who was close to President Johnson and who would, for many years to come, support the Vietnam War.

On the eve of the 1964 Summer Project, SNCC staff expressed their deep uneasiness with the idea of seeking to be seated at Atlantic City. The following are extracts from the minutes of the SNCC staff meeting June 9–11, 1964.[10]

Ruby Doris Smith opened a discussion on goals with the words: "We could begin with discussion of whether we're working to make basic changes within existing political and economic structures. . . . What would the seating of the delegation mean besides having Negroes in the National Democratic Party?" Here were some of the responses.

Ivanhoe Donaldson: Disagrees with just making more Democrats and more Republicans. Perhaps the way is to create a parallel structure. . . . Our problem is that our programs don't change basic factors of exploitation. Perhaps it's better to create a third stream. . . . [W]hat is the point of working within the Democratic Party? It is not a radical tool.

Charlie Cobb: Feels there would be negligible value in merely being part of the Democratic Party structure. . . . There is a danger of Negroes being manipulated by the national parties. . . . It is bad if you make people part of a decadent structure.

John Lewis: He is not sure that we can get what we want within "liberal politics." The basic things we want to achieve are equality for Negro and white, liberate the poor white as well as the Negro.

Jim Forman: We should agitate for dignity. . . . Dignity is an umbrella concept. E.g., a man without a job has no dignity.

Jim Jones: SNCC's program is limited to desegregating facilities and voter registration.

Lawrence Guyot: If our goal is just voter registration then we should stop. We have to organize around something.

---

10. Minutes from staff meeting, June 9–11, 1964, SNCC Papers, Roll 3, Frames 975–92. I wish to thank Wesley Hogan for making these minutes available to me.

In order to distinguish itself from the Mississippi regulars, the MFDP felt obliged to emphasize its fidelity to President Johnson and to the program of the national, as distinct from the state, Democratic Party. Organizing materials prepared by Donna Richards, Casey Hayden and other SNCC staff members for MFDP precinct and county meetings accordingly called for a "loyalty pledge" to the national Party.[11]

Further, in March 1964 Bob Moses and Ella Baker went to the national convention of the United Automobile Workers (UAW) and arranged for UAW attorney Joseph Rauh to represent the MFDP at Atlantic City. It seemed a logical move at the time. Rauh was an influential Democrat. The National Lawyers Guild attorneys who were doing the day-to-day legal work in Mississippi were *persona non grata* to many liberals in the national Democratic Party who perceived the Guild as Communist-dominated. No one imagined that a conflict could arise between the UAW, which had contributed heavily to the 1963 March for Jobs and Freedom, and the MFDP. As late as August 6, 1964, a summer volunteer wrote home "from the floor of the State Convention of the Mississippi Freedom Democratic Party": "Attorney Joseph Rauh . . . addressed the group. Mr. Rauh is also Walter Reuther's attorney and his appearance indicated the support of Mr. Reuther who is, of course, one of the powers of the Democratic Party."[12]

After James Chaney, Andrew Goodman, and Michael Schwerner disappeared, and had in all probability been murdered, it became much more difficult to continue the discussion begun at the SNCC staff meeting in June. On the one hand, national support for actually seating the MFDP delegates at the Democratic Party convention increased dramatically. On the other hand, a feeling grew in Mississippi that only if the delegates were seated would the sacrifice of Chaney, Goodman and Schwerner have been worthwhile.

Ms. Baker's course of conduct reflected these cross currents. According to her biographer, "Ella Baker was not surprised to

---

11. Casey Hayden, "Fields of Blue," in Constance Curry et al., *Deep in Our Hearts: Nine White Women in the Freedom Movement* (Athens, GA: University of Georgia Press, 2000), p. 357. I believe that such maneuvering took a toll. By the Waveland conference in November 1964, Casey felt "uninterested in electoral politics." Ibid., p. 367.

12. Quoted in *Letters from Mississippi*, edited and with a new preface by Elizabeth Sutherland Martinez (Brookline, MA: Zephyr Press, 2002), pp. 250–51.

discover that politicians and the civil rights leaders who looked to [the MFDP] to produce change were reluctant to embrace a grass-roots organization when it took an uncompromising stance."[13] Yet she became director of the party's office in Washington, DC, and "played an important role in coordinating the MFDP's national political strategy and in anchoring its northern-based lobbying effort."[14] When the buses arrived from Mississippi carrying MFDP delegates, Ms. Baker had arranged for the delegates to stay at a motel called the Gem. (It was not a "gem" but these rooms were all the MFDP's meager budget permitted.) Barbara Ransby sums up Baker's somewhat conflicting actions and perceptions this way:

> Even after she accepted the post of director of the MFDP's Washington office, Baker continued to harbor serious doubts about exactly what the MFDP contingent could manage to accomplish at the convention, and she certainly never expected an all-out victory. Yet she acted as if she were at least guardedly optimistic as plans for Atlantic City moved forward.[15]

Lyndon Johnson and Walter Reuther betrayed the hopes of the MFDP would-be delegates who had made the long bus trip from the South. Nelson Lichtenstein in his biography of Reuther, and Taylor Branch in his biography of Dr. King, tell the same story.[16]

At Johnson's request, Reuther broke off negotiations with GM and flew to Atlantic City by chartered plane. Arriving at 3 a.m. Reuther went into session with Hubert Humphrey and Walter Mondale. They agreed that the MFDP would be required to accept a so-called "compromise": the Mississippi regulars would continue to be the official delegation and the MFDP would have two "at large" delegates named by the president, who, so Humphrey made clear, would not include "that illiterate woman," Fannie Lou Hamer.

---

13. Ransby, *Ella Baker*, p. 334.
14. Ibid., p. 335.
15. Ibid., p. 336.
16. Nelson Lichtenstein, *The Most Dangerous Man in Detroit: Walter Reuther and the Fate of American Labor* (New York: Basic Books, 1995), pp. 394–95; Taylor Branch, *Pillar of Fire: America in the King Years, 1963–1965* (New York: Simon & Schuster, 1998), pp. 469–75.

Exhausted MFDP delegates instructed their attorney, Joseph Rauh, to hold out for at least the same number of seats allotted to the regulars. However, Reuther told Rauh, "Here's the decision. I am telling you to take this deal." Reuther added that if Rauh did not do what he was told, he would terminate Rauh's employment with the UAW.

The same kind of strongarm tactics were used with Dr. King. Reuther told him, "Your funding is on the line. The kind of money you got from us in Birmingham is there again for Mississippi, but you've got to help us and we've got to help Johnson."

The MFDP delegates rejected the so-called "compromise." Ms. Hamer told her fellow delegates from Mississippi that "we didn't come all this way for no two seats." No delegates of the Mississippi Freedom Democratic Party were seated.

After Atlantic City, Bayard Rustin and others still sought to persuade SNCC to look to its "coalition partners" for allies in confronting the economic and social structures that underpin racism in the United States. But precisely those allies—the national Democratic Party, and the allegedly most progressive trade union leader in the United States—had just finished conspiring against, and humiliating, the MFDP delegates at Atlantic City. As a result, many if not most of SNCC's African-American staff gave up on working within the system, working with organized labor, and working with whites.

Here is how Bob Moses put it at the Waveland conference:

Let's sum up the box we're in:
1) Labor unions are political organizations, now within the Establishment.
2) When labor is organized, it can only discuss a narrow aspect of the problem: wages. Reuther sat in the meeting with King, Humphrey and others to urge the FDP to accept the compromise, talking anti-Goldwater, keep morality out of politics, etc.[17]

SNCC failed to find a way out of the box described by Bob Moses. SNCC, after the mountaintop months of summer 1964,

---

17. Minutes, discussion of Nov. 9, 1964, SNCC Papers, Reel 11, Frames 935–99. Once again, I have Wesley Hogan to thank for the opportunity to see these records.

stumbled and failed to find a way forward. Explanations offered by historians stress a conflict of strategies. SNCC executive secretary Jim Forman wished to transform SNCC into what amounted to a Marxist-Leninist vanguard party, and to pursue voter registration in "Black Belt" counties across the South where blacks were a majority. Others, including Bob Moses and Casey Hayden, sought to continue decentralized grassroots activity in which organizers took direction from the people among whom they lived.[18]

I believe there is a simpler way to explain why SNCC's work in Mississippi and elsewhere fell apart after Atlantic City. If one can imagine such a thing as "organizing in a spirit of accompaniment," that is what characterized SNCC activity from 1960 through the summer of 1964. But after Atlantic City, SNCC people left.

Trying to Pick up the Pieces

In what follows I want to: 1) Look more closely at SNCC's only major initiative after 1964, the creation of the Lowndes County Freedom Organization in Lowndes County, Alabama; 2) Ask whether what happened in Lowndes County reveals a more general failing in the "organizing" undertaken by the movements of the 1960s, as in the Economic Research and Action Project (ERAP) of the Students for a Democratic Society; and 3) Examine the SNCC strategy in projecting "Black Power" and to ask where we now find ourselves.

1. The Lowndes County Freedom Organization

After the drama of the Mississippi Summer Project and the trauma of the national Democratic Party convention, a number of seasoned SNCC activists relocated to Lowndes County in central Alabama. Thanks to a fine book by Hasan Kwame Jeffries, *Bloody Lowndes: Civil Rights and Black Power in Alabama's Black Belt* (New York: New York University Press, 2009), we can follow what happened in detail.

---

18. Compare James Forman, *The Making of Black Revolutionaries* (Seattle: Open Hand Publishing, 1985), with Wesley Hogan, *Many Minds, One Heart: SNCC's Dreams for a New America* (Chapel Hill: University of North Carolina Press, 2007).

SNCC's project director in Lowndes County was Stokely Carmichael. He and other Mississippi veterans gravitated to Alabama because, after Atlantic City, they were "interested in working outside the Democratic Party." Their experience during the Summer Project also caused them to oppose interracial projects. At the end of the summer project, an unexpectedly large number of white summer volunteers opted to stay on in Mississippi and decision-making in local organizing projects became problematic. (There is a remarkably precise parallelism between the trajectories of SNCC and the Zapatistas in this respect. For several years after the Zapatista insurrection began in 1994, well-intentioned volunteers from all over the world flooded the struggling indigenous communities of Chiapas. The Zapatistas finally decided that, except in special cases, volunteers should stay for no more than six weeks. This was also the approximate length of the 1964 Mississippi Summer Project.)

African-American SNCC organizers began their work in Lowndes County during the famous Selma to Montgomery march in late March 1965. According to Carmichael, "We trailed that march. Every time local folks came out, we'd sit and talk with them, get their names, find out where they lived, their addresses, what church, who their ministers were, like that. So all the information, everything you'd need to organize, we got."

There followed laborious and dangerous door-to-door canvassing. A mass meeting, with the specific purpose of recruiting volunteers to try to register to vote the next day, attracted five hundred people to Mt. Gilliard church. At first the local movement called itself the Lowndes County Christian Movement for Human Rights. Then it became the Lowndes County Freedom Organization, and adopted the logo of a Black Panther.

By May 1965, hundreds of African Americans, dressed in their best Sunday clothes, were lining up outside the county jail twice a month in Hayneville to try to register. A lawsuit was filed, a couple of hundred people volunteering to be plaintiffs. Lowndes County registrars met secretly with a U.S. attorney, and agreed to drop the literacy portion of the registration application and to keep the registrar's office open for four consecutive days in July. Nonetheless, persistent defiance by local registrars in refusing to register applicants for technical reasons finally caused the Justice Department, acting pursuant to the new federal Voting Rights Act, to send federal registrars. "Although registering remained economically risky and physically dangerous, by the end of October 1965 some two thousand African Americans, or 40 percent of the black electorate, had become eligible voters."

In May 1966, the Lowndes County freedom movement held a nominating convention. Eligible voters were directed to seven tables where each was handed a slip of paper displaying the names of potential nominees, the phrase "One Man, One Vote," and the Black Panther logo of the Lowndes County Freedom Organization.

In November 1966, the first local election in which there was mass African-American participation was held. Black candidates trailed their white opponents by several hundred votes but, in a locality where African Americans were an overwhelming majority, the eventual electoral success of the Lowndes County Freedom Organization seemed assured.

Shortly after the 1966 election, however, the organization withdrew its staff although SNCC had been in Lowndes County less than two years. Why did they do this? The answer is that SNCC was following the prevailing organizing doctrine of the 1960s, practiced by labor unions, by white as well as black movements, and by community organizations. Chuck McDew, SNCC's first chairperson,

> explained that many SNCC staffers had always viewed the committee as a short-lived group of organizers who would eventually organize themselves out of a job. "We said that if we go more than five years or if we go without an understanding or feeling that the organization would be disbanded, we will run the risk of becoming institutionalized and spending more time trying to perpetuate the institution than having the freedom to act and do."[19]

Stokely Carmichael offered precisely the same reason for leaving Lowndes County after staying there so briefly:

> Our way is to live in the community, find, train, or develop representative leadership within strong, accountable local organizations or coalitions that did not exist before, and that are capable of carrying on the struggle after we leave.

---

19. Hogan, *Many Minds*, pp. 221, 375 n. 8.

When we succeed in this, we will work ourselves out of a
job. Which is our goal.[20]

Thus the trade union organizing model, initially imitated by community organizer Saul Alinsky, was passed on to the young people
of the New Left.

But in Lowndes County, SNCC's withdrawal did not work out
as Stokely Carmichael had hoped. After another electoral defeat
by about the same margin as in 1966, the leaders of the Lowndes
County Freedom Organization decided to drop the Black Panther
logo. They successfully advocated at a mass meeting that the local
party should merge with a statewide African-American party that
supported the Democratic Party's national candidates. John Hulett,
longtime leader of the Lowndes County movement, began to cut
deals with his white counterparts without authorization from the
party rank and file. And not long after the 1972 election, Hulett
decided to join the Democratic Party.

Professor Jeffries draws a number of lessons from the miscarriage
of movement electoral politics in Alabama. He says that movement
activists believed that political power was the key to progress, but
electing African Americans to office failed to produce sweeping
changes. Activists underestimated structural impediments to racial
equality. For example, it simply was not possible under existing state
law "to tax the rich to feed the poor." Movement activists also assumed that people would continue to adhere to the tenets of freedom
politics once outside organizers left the scene. In fact, "popular interest in freedom politics waned as soon as movement activists stopped
doing political education work." In sum, "[o]ver-investing in elected
officials and the Democratic Party kept African Americans from developing new grassroots leaders."[21]

Piven and Cloward, in their survey of the civil rights movement, emphatically agree. "The crucial question," they wrote in 1977,
was "whether the winning of formal political rights will now enable
blacks to progress economically." They were concerned that:

> The election of a modest number of southern black officials
> will clearly not create the political power necessary to secure

---

20. Jeffries, *Bloody Lowndes*, p. 213.
21. Ibid., pp. 243–45.

national full employment policies; nor to secure substantial changes in the hiring and wage and promotion policies of private industry; nor the huge subsidies required to house the southern urban minority poor decently; nor any measures, such as land reform coupled with federal subsidies, that might enable some of the rural black (and white) poor to remain in independent farming in an era of agribusiness; nor reform of the welfare system to insure an adequate minimum income for all who cannot or should not work; nor any one of a dozen other policies and programs that might improve the living conditions of the black poor.

The black vote, Piven and Cloward concluded, was not likely to bring about necessary structural economic change for African Americans. Such change would more likely result from "the eruption of a new period of mass defiance."[22]

2. The SDS Economic Research and Action Project (ERAP)

In conscious imitation of the work of their black counterparts in the South, in 1963 the Students for a Democratic Society (SDS) created organizing projects in a number of Northern cities. They did so, moreover, with a considered and articulated economic analysis and a strategic economic program. The SDS analysis was that structural contradictions in the American capitalist economy would give rise to mass unemployment, that unemployment would afflict both white and black jobseekers, and that SDS members should consider leaving the college campus, moving to an inner city, and helping to organize "an interracial movement of the poor."

The packet of materials assembled for prospective Freedom School teachers in 1964 included a reprint from *Liberation* magazine entitled "The Triple Revolution" in which one of the expected revolutions was said to be unemployment caused by automation. SDSers were well aware that in Northern cities the right to vote existed at least in theory and that a radical movement would face problems different from those that SNCC had targeted in the South. On the basis of their experience in nearby Cambridge, Maryland, Swarthmore

---

22. Frances Fox Piven and Richard Cloward, *Poor People's Movements: Why They Succeed, How They Fail* (New York: Pantheon Books, 1977), pp. 256–58.

College students Carl Wittman and Vernon Grizzard wrote a paper in which they asserted that economic inequality was at the heart of oppression in the North. The South, they wrote, "was on its way to becoming a tokenly desegregated society with poor housing, poor schools, and unemployment as the model, as the North now is." They went on to say, "It is increasingly clear that the main problem of Cambridge is not the race problem—for that is only exacerbated by the real problem: poverty and increasingly serious unemployment." The two young men commented further that "one problem with the South is that they can be satisfied so easily." Equal access to public accommodations could be granted "without the whites having to give much at all." In a few years, the South might be desegregated enough "to satisfy civil rights organizations, but not enough to solve the problems of poor schools and unemployment."[23]

This paper, written in 1963, was elaborated by Wittman and Tom Hayden a year later in a better-known document entitled "An Interracial Movement of the Poor?" Likewise in the first part of 1964 Mario Savio, together with other students in Berkeley in the local University Friends of SNCC chapter, organized a sit-in at the Sheraton Palace hotel in San Francisco that demanded changes in the hiring practices of a hotel that employed few blacks and only in the most me-nial, low-paying jobs. Retrospectively, Savio "highlighted the implicit anticapitalism of the civil rights protests, pointing out that the move-ment insisted that stores, hotels, and other commercial establishments elevate political morality above profitability, hiring minorities whether or not their presence might turn away prejudiced white customers."[24]

Tom Hayden located himself in central Newark and helped to organize the relatively successful Newark Community Union Project. Newark was a major Northern city in which African Americans were the majority of the population.

Another important ERAP project, in which former SDS presi-dent Todd Gitlin, Michael James, and Rennie Davis participated, was in a poor white neighborhood on the north side of Chicago. The project generated the slogan "Jobs Or Income Now" and became known as the JOIN project. Todd Gitlin remembered that this project grew out of a suggestion by Stokely Carmichael. As he would later

---

23. Hogan, *Many Minds*, pp. 128, 336 n. 28.
24. Robert Cohen, *Freedom's Orator: Mario Savio and the Radical Legacy of the 1960s* (New York: Oxford University Press, 2009), pp. 42–45, 47.

famously propose as the new chairperson of SNCC in 1966, in 1963 Carmichael suggested at an SDS meeting in Bloomington, Indiana, that SDS go out into the community and organize poor whites.

But the mass unemployment predicted by SDS analysis did not come to pass in the 1960s because of the Vietnam War. "[T]he issue of jobs failed to mobilize significant numbers of neighborhood residents. . . . [T]he rate of unemployment was on the decline; it averaged just above 5 percent over the decade. . . . 'Just as we got to Chicago,' Lee Webb remembered, 'lines at the unemployment compensation center started to get shorter.'"[25]

ERAP organizers Tom Hayden and Rennie Davis withdrew from community organizing and turned to antiwar work. Hayden traveled to Hanoi with me in December 1965, and Davis and other SDS representatives met with delegates from the National Liberation Front of South Vietnam in Bratislava, Czechoslovakia, in late summer 1967. The two then devoted years of their lives to persistent agitation against the war.

Did ERAP fail? Yes, in that none of the SDS projects were able to organize successfully around the economic issues they had determined to be crucial, and all the projects went out of existence after a few years. But perhaps in a longer perspective it did not, inasmuch as the United States now finds itself confronted by stubborn structural unemployment like that projected half a century ago. The cause of structural unemployment in the twenty-first century may not be the automation on which analysis focused in the early 1960s. But the availability of low-wage workers in other countries, inducing corporations in the United States to close plants in this country and locate new capital investment elsewhere, produces the result anticipated half a century ago.

One of the largest employers in the Youngstown area is a company formerly known as Packard Electric (now Delphi Packard). It makes electric components, primarily for General Motors. When the Lynds moved to this part of the world in the 1970s, there were close to fifteen thousand workers employed at Packard Electric plants in the Mahoning Valley and none in Mexico. Today there are only a few hundred Packard employees left in the Youngstown area. Meantime,

---

25. Jennifer Frost, *"An Interracial Movement of the Poor": Community Organizing and the New Left in the 1960s* (New York and London: New York University Press, 2001), pp. 96–97.

Packard has become the largest multinational corporation in Mexico with over forty thousand workers.

To whatever extent the ERAP analysis was wrong because the analysis took much longer to materialize than expected, another consideration comes into play. Like Stokely Carmichael in Lowndes County, the ERAP organizers in Northern inner cities did not stay very long. Indeed Northern Student Movement activist Peter Countryman at one point wrote to SNCC staff member Tim Jenkins that there was needed a group of people who would "for two months live in one room apartments and eat hamburgers and . . . sustain the necessary sacrifice, and go into that community, and talk the language of the people and be sensitive to their problems."[26]

Two months? Even two years? This was the monumental fallacy of believing that one could enter a new situation in which one was a total stranger, very likely live together with other "organizers" in a Freedom House unlike anything ever before experienced in the neighborhood, offer local residents no discernible professional expertise such as a teacher, a doctor, or a lawyer might provide, leave after two months or two years, and expect to bring about revolutionary social change.

SDS activists in the inner cities of the North, like the great majority of their SNCC colleagues in the Deep South, failed to stay in the communities where they were organizing for more than two or three years. As Jennifer Frost concludes her definitive study of ERAP:

> [N]ot enough New Left organizers understood or appreciated community organizing . . . as the slow, undramatic, and long-term process of helping people develop their powers . . . New Left participants failed to adopt a model for lifelong organizing. Most followed SNCC's example of young people "dropping out" from schools or careers for a few years of full-time organizing. . . . ERAP failed to develop a model of organizing . . . they could sustain over the long haul. Instead their approach led to exhaustion and "burnout."

Eric Mann, an ERAP volunteer in Newark, belatedly came to the insight that what was needed was the "long-distance runner thing."[27]

---

26. Hogan, *Many Minds*, p. 136.
27. Frost, *Interracial Movement*, pp. 174–75.

3. Black and White Together

After the Atlantic City convention, African-American members of
SNCC began to develop a "Black Power" perspective. In presenting
it to their white associates, they said it was a short-term strategy. They
represented that their concern was to extricate African Americans
from situations in which they might tend to defer to more articulate
Caucasians. In fall 1964, this was a problem in many Mississippi projects
where white summer volunteers had remained in much larger numbers
than originally expected. For the time being, SNCC projected, white
activists should devote their energies to organizing poor and working-
class whites. Then we would all come back together, uniting blacks and
whites in a single renewed Movement for fundamental social change.
In the long run, we would still be "black and white together."

At least this is how I remember it. There are fragments of
memory that are painful to recall and apparently contradictory. At
the Waveland conference in early November 1964, I approached an
African-American SNCC staff member who had been very much
involved in developing the Freedom School program, as was I. He
completely ignored me. Later on, however, Stokely Carmichael spoke
in New Haven and went out of his way to say that in promoting Black
Power he did not intend to detract from his sense of comradeship with
Staughton Lynd, or words to that effect. In the summer of 1965, Bob
Moses and I were arrested together as we protested the Vietnam War,
and I recall a conversation with him in which he said that he could
not seem to find solid ground under his feet in the peace movement.
But not long afterward, Bob stopped returning my telephone calls.

Others seem to have had similar tangled moments.

Faith Holsaert recalls that three years before Willie Ricks and
Stokely popularized the words "Black Power" during the Meredith
march in 1966, Ricks was arrested in Albany, Georgia, and assigned
to sweep street trash outside the SNCC office. When he saw other
SNCC staff, "[a] slow grin spread over his face. . . . [H]e shot his fist
into the air, yelling 'Black Power!'"[28]

Denise Nicholas worked with the Free Southern Theater and
remembers that it "had always been a mixed group, and there were a
couple of white people who had been integral to making this project

---

28. *Hands on the Freedom Plow: Personal Accounts by Women in SNCC*, ed.
Faith S. Holsaert et al. (Urbana: University of Illinois Press, 2010), p. 191.

happen. People you'd come to know and love were suddenly being excluded."[29]

Martha Prescod Norman Noonan writes that she always understood SNCC to be a black Freedom Movement, led by blacks. Whites, and Northerners whether white or black, had a voice but not a vote. "To this day I don't know what the logic was that said it was necessary to break off relations with our white associates."[30]

Penny Patch says that she never had a problem with Black Power as a political concept. "It was the exclusion that hurt so bad." But no matter what came after, "there was a brief time when we were black and white together."[31]

The leadership of SNCC had always been African American. Emmie Schrader Adams reflects, correctly I think: "Had the number of whites remained at about ten to twenty, spread thinly over the project areas and not concentrated in the seats of power, there would have been no contradiction to the agenda of Black Power."[32]

But that, as it turned out, was not to be, and within a few years the vision of recreating an interracial Movement had been forgotten. It does not exist to this day.

Nevertheless, there have been historical moments when ordinary workers, combat soldiers in Vietnam, and high security prisoners, acted out SNCC's idea that blacks and whites would first organize separately, and then come together to change the world.

Alice and I interviewed an Indiana truck driver named George Sullivan for our book *Rank and File*.[33] Like David Roediger, author of *Wages of Whiteness*, George grew up in southern Illinois. His childhood was saturated with racism:

> There never was any question in my mind that niggers weren't any good. The one thing I never knew anyone to worry about was problems with the niggers. There weren't any around where I lived.

---

29. Ibid., p. 264.
30. Ibid., p. 501.
31. Constance Curry et al., *Deep in Our Hearts: Nine White Women in the Freedom Movement* (Athens: University of Georgia Press, 2000), pp. 163, 170.
32. Ibid., p. 330.
33. George Sullivan, "Working for Survival," in *Rank and File*, ed. Lynd and Lynd (expanded edition), pp. 208–9.

One did come to the house one time, scared me to death. I saw him at the door, there he was, and I didn't know what to do. Any time we would be doing something wrong, one of the comments my mother would make was, "I'll have some big nigger come and get you if you don't stop that."

All this changed when George went into military service. He was first assigned to a barracks with seventy or seventy-five whites and three blacks. Then he was transferred to a new base. He arrived at midday, went to the barracks to which he was assigned, put his gear on a bed, and went to the canteen. Returning about three-thirty or four, he "didn't see a white face. It was a barracks full of black people."

George says that he "knew, of course, that the sergeant had made an error, put me in the wrong barracks. So I went to the headquarters and told him he'd made a mistake." The sergeant explained that there was a new policy of integration and as white men came on the base they would be put in the same barracks. "You just happen to be the first."

For the first few days "I didn't talk to any of them," George continues. "They didn't talk to me. . . . They didn't know how to deal with [the first white man in the barracks] any more than I knew how to deal with them."

Then came an experience that illustrates an argument made by Howard Zinn in his book *The Southern Mystique.* Howard thought that everyone has a hierarchy of values. Racism may well be one of them but it is unlikely to be the thing that anyone cares about most. Change the external requirements of daily life so that whites must engage in equal status contact with blacks in order to achieve their highest priorities, and over time, attitudes will change in response.[34]

George Sullivan had anticipated that his barracks would be racially segregated. He was accustomed to such segregation. No doubt he would have said that he preferred it.

But George was on the verge of "making sergeant," a higher priority. He had been working as a meat cutter, had cut three or four of his fingers, and couldn't use one of his hands. He had just been

---

34. Howard Zinn, *The Southern Mystique* (New York: Alfred A. Knopf, 1964), pp. 18 ("you *first* change the way people behave . . . in order to transform the environment which is the ultimate determinant of the way they think"), 93 ("the universal detergent for race prejudice is *contact*—massive, prolonged, equal, and intimate contact").

promoted to sergeant but could not sew on his new stripes. As he was sitting on the barracks steps, wondering what to do, an officer came by and told him, "You'll have stripes on your uniform by tomorrow or we'll take them away from you."

One of the guys in the barracks "had heard the conversation. He came out and said, 'Have you already got your stripes?'" Yes, said George, but I can't sew with one hand. "He said, 'Well, if you go get them I'll sew them on for you.' So that was the first thing that really broke the ice. He sat and sewed those stripes on my uniform while we got to know each other."

The experience of combat soldiers in Vietnam as described by Richard Moser is an almost comical instance of the process SNCC envisioned: first people organize in their separate groups, then they unite for joint action. Moser's extensive research indicated that soldiers organized themselves into "buddy groups" of three kinds: heads, juicers, and brothers. The heads were into Jefferson Airplane, or Janis Joplin, or Jimi Hendrix. The juicers "would be more into country music." As for the brothers, they "were like into their own thing." But there was "sort of a common bond" because a certain percentage of black guys were also smoking pot, and in that period, "rock music incorporated soul music."

Long hair, peace signs, hippie beads, and pot smoking became commonplace among the heads. The brothers would not pass each other without exchanging the Black Power salute. They wore black arm bands that had been woven from shoe laces and used a black solidarity handshake, or "dap."

Gathered into these separate buddy groups, hippies, Appalachians, blacks, and Hispanics nevertheless acted together against a war perceived by all to be meaningless.[35]

Finally, the supermax prison, conventionally perceived as a snakepit of gang hostilities, also offers dramatic instances of class solidarity overcoming racial separation.[36]

The key at Attica and at Lucasville was for members of each race first to organize separately, with whatever music, dress, and

35. See Richard Moser, *The New Winter Soldiers: GI and Veteran Dissent during the Vietnam Era* (New Brunswick: Rutgers University Press, 1996), especially chapter 3.
36. See Staughton Lynd, *Lucasville: The Untold Story of a Prison Uprising* (Oakland, CA: PM Press, 2011), especially chapter 7.

symbolism spoke to each group's particular culture, and then unite and fight. Separation in the first stages of group activity was a necessary *tactic*. (In the words of an Aryan Brotherhood leader in Ohio, "If you have two men in a cell and one is into country and the other is into soul music, you've got a problem.") But the *strategy* was racial solidarity on behalf of common goals.

In Vietnam and in American prisons these bonds of "black and white together" formed under the hammer of common danger and oppression. It remains to be seen whether the same process can bring together African Americans, Caucasians, and Hispanics when they are in civilian life rather than in a war zone, or on the street instead of behind bars.

I believe that whether we succeed in creating a new, interracial movement of poor and working people depends on first recognizing the need for this two-step process. The formation of identity in groups of African Americans, or Aryans, or women, or gays, or any other identifiable minority, is a stage and a tactic that must be followed by creation of a united movement. Subgroups should feel free to gather by themselves as needed but the purpose of forming a new, united Movement must be recognized as paramount by all.

A Final Comment

Looking back, it is clear to me that SNCC hastened its demise by ignoring the need for an economic program. At several gatherings in early 1964, I tried to urge SNCC staffers to give some thought to this. I said that today's movement had to have something comparable to the demand for forty acres and a mule after the Civil War. I argued that the programmatic perspective needed was like a stool that required three legs: the vote; federal marshals to protect African Americans in registering to vote; but also, a program to help blacks in the Deep South find their way beyond desperate poverty and economic dependence. I was told that I wanted SNCC to have an "ideology."

I still think that such an economic program was indispensable. At the crucial Waveland conference in November 1964, SNCC executive secretary Jim Forman advocated an expanded registration campaign in the "Black Belt" counties where African Americans had historically been a majority. But at that very moment, the introduction of the mechanical cotton picker was destroying the livelihood of black sharecroppers in the Mississippi Delta, prompting migration to the North. This migration, of course, changed the demographic balance and lessened the possibility that African Americans could use the ballot to make fundamental changes in Southern society.

Accompaniment

Against the War

THE MOVEMENT AGAINST THE WAR IN VIETNAM WAS A FABRIC OF many strands. There were rallies, beginning with a gathering of about twenty-five thousand people in Washington, DC, in April 1965, and swelling to occasions that brought hundreds of thousands into the streets. There were individual actions as when Daniel Ellsberg reproduced and distributed the Pentagon Papers, or Norman Morrison set fire to himself outside the Pentagon. There were protest marches, like the assemblage on those same Pentagon steps in October 1967, when student activists overcame their hostility toward young men like themselves in uniform, put flowers in the rifle barrels of the soldiers who confronted them, and called out, "Join us!" And there were activities such as refusal to register for the draft, the creation of coffee houses adjacent to military bases, and the return of medals and decorations by veterans who threw these emblems of glory over the White House fence.

"Organizing" and nonviolent "accompaniment" were interwoven, over and over again, in complex patterns, throughout this history. Yet in contrast to the labor movement, to community organizing, and even to the Southern civil rights movement, the movement against the Vietnam War came down in the end to the actions of individuals who refused to fight, and other individuals who supported them. One cannot "organize" a conscientious refusal to go to war. One can stimulate that refusal by one's own exemplary actions, and by "accompanying" such acts, for example by draft counseling.

Accompanying War Objectors (by Alice Lynd)

Anti–Vietnam War activists commemorated the destruction of Hiroshima and Nagasaki on August 6–9, 1965, twenty years after those cities were devastated by the first use of atomic bombs, by the United States. An Assembly of Unrepresented People came together in Washington, DC, first in workshops on the mall and then to declare peace with the people of Vietnam.

I attended a workshop sponsored by the Central Committee for Conscientious Objectors. Counselors were needed for men who did not want to be drafted for service in Vietnam. I asked whether I could become a draft counselor. "If you could get anyone to come to you," I was told. "There is one woman who does it."

Getting people to come to me was not a problem. We lived only five blocks from Yale University and Staughton was already well known as an opponent of the Vietnam War.

One evening in the fall of 1966, a group of divinity students met in our home. Divinity students were exempt from the draft. Some of them felt that they should not enjoy a privilege that was unavailable to other young men. I recall a woman who was there that night saying she knew a man who had gone to prison rather than register for the draft, and she thought he regretted it. We knew the man to whom she was referring, and I thought, "I wonder what Tom would say." After the meeting ended, I suggested to Staughton that he should write a book about what particular war resisters had done, why, and how they felt about it. Staughton replied that I, not he, should do it. "I'll help you," he said.

I, sometimes we, began to go to gatherings of war resisters in New York and Chicago. Lawyers working with war resisters gave me relevant papers. I put a notice in *New Left Notes*, the newspaper of Students for a Democratic Society (SDS), asking for "Dear Draft Board" letters and other statements and accounts by men who were refusing to serve. I collected leaflets. I read diaries. I looked for a range of different actions and reasons for refusing military service. Some men refused to register. Some sought to be recognized as conscientious objectors, but that classification was limited to men who could persuade their local draft board that they objected to participation in war in any form for reasons of religious training and belief. Some men objected to participation in the Vietnam War, or in wars that violated international law. Some men went into the military but refused a particular assignment. Some went to prison. Three of the accounts were by wives of men who refused military service. I never could read those accounts without crying. I wondered how, young as they were, they could have been so strong.

In 1968, as draft calls were escalating, my book was published.[1] By that time, we had moved from New Haven to Chicago. The Central Committee for Conscientious Objectors was opening an

---

1. Alice Lynd, *We Won't Go: Personal Accounts of War Objectors* (Boston: Beacon Press, 1968).

office in Chicago, and I was hired by the Midwest Committee for Draft Counselors to train draft counselors. That was difficult for me. I much preferred doing the draft counseling, rather than writing memos about how to do it. Instead of going systematically through the grounds and requirements for each classification, I revamped the curriculum: what are the first questions a counselor needs to ask the counselee?

After about a year, I changed jobs. I became the coordinator of draft counseling for the Chicago area in the regional office of the American Friends Service Committee. It was my job to be sure that before a man refused induction into military service he had done everything that could be done to prepare for a lawyer to take the case. I also set up occasions where an inexperienced counselor could bring a counselee for counseling by one of the most experienced counselors in the area. If a technical question arose, we would look at the appropriate regulation or official memorandum.

I think the experienced counselors learned the most. It was as if the more we knew, the more we learned from each other. We would listen to how the counselor phrased the question that opened up what needed to be said. Or, after the counseling was done, one of us might ask another counselor, "What were you driving at when you asked such-and-such a question?"

Draft counseling was not limited to counselees who objected to military service for reasons of conscience. We provided information concerning medical deferments, or hardship claims. The Chicago Area Draft Resisters (CADRE) tried to reach out to working-class youth. Members of CADRE particularly scorned what they called "mind-bending." If someone is going to refuse the draft he had better do it for his own reasons, not as the result of pressure from someone else, because it is he who will have to take the consequences. The draft counselor asks questions and provides information that may help the counselee to decide what he wants to do and how to do it.

I ran into that problem with lawyers and law students. A lawyer might want to try some new legal theory. And the draft resister would say, "If I have to go to prison, I want to make my own statement, not his." Members of CADRE, including female supporters of draft resisters, took care of each other. They had pot luck suppers that we sometimes attended. A theme song of the Resistance was "Amazing Grace."

Every Wednesday night we had an open house at our home where people came to talk together about the issues with which they were struggling, such as, "Is nonviolence a tactic or a way of life?" "How effective would [this or that tactic] be" in stopping the war? Some said, "Regardless of effectiveness, I can do no other than refuse to go."

In retrospect it seems that, although we never thought of the word, what we were doing was accompanying. We did not offer any program or presentation. We provided space for people to come together and explore a shared concern.

Conscientious Objection in a Volunteer Army (by Staughton Lynd)

As the Vietnam War drew to a close, the U.S. government concluded that it never again wanted to conscript young men (or women) to fight a long war with heavy casualties. Vietnam appeared to prove that such an army in such a war gave rise to too much insubordination and unrest. Richard Moser, in his book *The New Winter Soldiers*, describes how soldiers in Vietnam came together in buddy groups of "heads," "juicers," and "brothers," and then joined in common action to help each other make it home alive.[2] By 1973, according to Tod Ensign, an alarmed military analyst stated, "Our army that remains in Vietnam is in a state approaching collapse, with individual units avoiding or having refused combat, murdering their officers[,] drug ridden and dispirited, where not mutinous."[3]

A soldier related that, "They have separate companies for men who refuse to go out into the field. It is no big thing to refuse to go." An infantry officer commented, "You can't give them an order and expect them to obey immediately. They ask why, and you have to tell them." *Time* magazine reported that officers were typically given two warnings before being fragged.[4]

Meantime in the States, activists began to approach soldiers with the invitation, "Join us." A young man who called himself "Superjoel" recalled how he acted out this invitation at the Pentagon in 1967:

---

2. Moser, *The New Winter Soldiers*, chapter 3.
3. Tod Ensign, "Who Serves?" in Mary Susannah Robbins, *Peace Not Terror: Leaders of the U.S. Antiwar Movement Speak Out Against U.S. Foreign Policy Post 9/11* (Lanham, MD: Lexington Books, 2008), p. 110.
4. Tom Wells, *The War Within: America's Battle over Vietnam* (Berkeley: University of California Press, 1994), p. 474.

I was between Abbie [Hoffman] and Dr. Spock. We're walking upon the grounds of the Pentagon. And on top of this pile of trash there's this bunch of flowers, daisies, right. I grabbed them. I saw these soldiers, and they're all standing there and they were my age. So I just took the flowers and one by one, boom, boom, boom, put 'em in the gun barrels.[5]

Coffee houses were opened near military bases in the United States, Germany, and Okinawa. An estimated 145 publications by and for GIs were created, ranging from newspapers with sophisticated graphics to mimeographed single sheets.[6] One survey reports that the number of men claiming conscientious objection rose from 18,000 in 1964 to 61,000 in 1971. Correspondingly, between 1965 and 1972 the number of federal prosecutions for draft evasion rose from 340 a year to nearly 5,000, and the average prison sentence for convicted evaders increased as well.[7]

Creating a Volunteer Army

One way out of the government's dilemma was to delegate the actual fighting to the young men of client states such as South Korea and South Vietnam. The prototype for this ineffectual strategy was so-called "Vietnamization" under President Nixon.

A second approach has been to pick fights only with other governments that could be easily and quickly defeated, such as Grenada, Panama, Lebanon, and Serbia. Then came Iraq (twice) and Afghanistan, where the armies of existing governments were quickly overwhelmed even when those defeats were followed by prolonged civil war. In the 1960s, SDS talked about addressing the structural problems of American society so that we would not, decades hence, find ourselves fighting what we called "the seventh war from now." Count them.

Vietnamization and picking on enemies that are small and weak are at best partial strategies for dispelling the so-called "Vietnam

---

5. Larry Sloman, *Steal This Dream: Abbie Hoffman and the Countercultural Revolution Against America* (New York: Doubleday, 1998), p. 98.
6. Ensign, "Who Serves?" pp. 110–11.
7. James W. Tollefson, *The Strength Not to Fight: An Oral History of Conscientious Objectors of the Vietnam War* (Boston: Little, Brown and Company, 2003), pp. 6–7.

syndrome." A third approach, alas somewhat more effective, has been for the armed forces increasingly to rely on technically advanced weapons activated from high in the air or in the case of drones from invulnerable command centers located far away from the battlefield. But even these super-weapons cannot altogether take the place of boots on the ground, as the war in Afghanistan has proved.

It was foreseeable that neither using somebody else's youth for combat, picking easy targets, or developing nonhuman means of attack would be sufficient. Well before the Vietnam War ended, the government concluded that it needed an all-volunteer army: an army of individuals who initially chose to fight rather than an army of people forced to do so.

A commission to "develop a comprehensive plan for eliminating conscription and moving toward an all-volunteer force" was created by President Nixon two months after taking office. According to Tod Ensign, the Nixon White House enlisted legendary Oklahoma football coach Bud Wilkinson to sell the idea to the public. Members of the commission included Milton Friedman and Alan Greenspan, who saw in a volunteer military a desirable product of the free play of market forces. The commission also included NAACP president Roy Wilkins, who may have anticipated what turned out to be the case: that African Americans, disproportionately vulnerable to economic hard times, would become a disproportionate part of the volunteer military. And stalwarts of the antiwar movement such as Benjamin Spock, Coretta Scott King, and George McGovern all supported the proposal for a volunteer force.[8]

The volunteer army came into being on July 1, 1973.

Accompanying Volunteer Objectors

A first question that we must ask and answer is: can a person who has volunteered for military service become a bona fide objector to further service on the basis of conscience?

If "conscience" is defined in the constricted manner of present laws and regulations the answer is, very rarely. Present laws and regulations require a member of the armed forces who claims Conscientious Objector status, first, to object to *participation in war in any form*, and second, to do so on the basis of *religious training and*

---

8. Ensign, "Who Serves?" pp. 115–17.

belief. Some soldiers like former Marine Carl Mirra have successfully done so. But it is obviously unlikely that many members of a
volunteer army will be able to say No to further service on the basis
of objection to any and all wars. The courts have modified what is
required in the way of proving religious belief but there has been no
change in the requirement that a CO must object to participation
in *all* wars.

There are also obstacles within the traditional movement against
war, inside our own heads and hearts. There is a tendency to devalue
and regard as insincere service men and women who refuse to fight
only after actually experiencing war crimes in combat. There is a
temptation to ask: why didn't they read the Sermon on the Mount
and listen to what their ministers said in church, synagogue, or
mosque before they volunteered?

Existing laws and regulations constitute a classic example of
what Herbert Marcuse called "repressive tolerance." At present,
only individuals who are members of groups such as the Quakers,
Mennonites, Amish, Church of the Brethren, and Jehovah's
Witnesses are likely to qualify as conscientious objectors to war. The
system implicitly declares: "Let them clean bed pans and plant pine
trees rather than serve in the military. The war machine does not need
these few persons."

In reality, it can be just as much an act of conscience to refuse to
commit war crimes in a particular war as to refuse to take part in all
wars. A human being who has actually been to war may experience
a more profound revulsion to further combat than a person who has
merely read the Bible and regularly gone to church. Accompaniment,
whether by a fellow soldier or by a person from the "other side," often
plays a critical role. Consider a few examples.

My friend and comrade, the late Howard Zinn, was an eager
volunteer for World War II. Working in a shipyard that made battle-
ships and landingcraft, he gave up a deferment that would have lasted
throughout the war and volunteered for the Air Corps. A program
known as "volunteering for induction" called for his local draft board
to send him an induction notice. "To make absolutely sure," Howard
writes, "I asked the draft board clerk if I could mail the induction notice myself, and I dropped it into the mailbox just outside the office."[9]

9. For all that follows, see Howard Zinn, *You Can't Be Neutral on a Moving Train: A Personal History of Our Times* (Boston: Beacon Press, 1994), pp. 93–95.

Once in military service, Howard Zinn did badly as an apprentice pilot but scored very well on tests for navigator and bombardier. He arranged to switch places with two other trainees so that he could become a bombardier as soon as possible. Then came the following experience.

> I'd made friends with a gunner on another crew. . . . [W]e were both readers, and we were both interested in politics. At a certain point he startled me by saying, "You know, this is not a war against fascism. . . . It's an imperialist war."

Howard asked his friend, "Then why are you here?" The answer was, "To talk to guys like you."

Howard Zinn's friend was apparently a member of the Socialist Workers Party. Its policy was to send eligible members into military service so as to engage other young soldiers like Howard in reconsidering support for the war. "Two weeks after that conversation," Howard recalled, "his plane . . . was shot down and his whole crew killed."

Howard was troubled by this conversation and never forgot it. "I didn't realize myself to what extent my mind was changing during the war," he says, but when it was over, he wrote "Never Again" on the folder holding his discharge papers.

Surely the young gunner had successfully accompanied his companion, the young bombardier. Howard Zinn was not then and never became a pacifist.[10] But no person more categorically and passionately condemned U.S. wars of aggression, the deception practiced by all governments to promote their wars, and the inevitability that any modern war would involve bombing, and the indiscriminate destruction of civilians, especially children, whom the bombardier can neither see, nor hear, nor smell.

When Brian Willson graduated from high school he wanted to become an FBI agent.[11] In the mid-1960s he volunteered for the

---

10. E.g., *Howard Zinn on War*, second edition (New York: Seven Stories Press, 2011), pp. 15–18.
11. For the following paragraphs see Brian Willson, *On Third World Legs* (Chicago: Charles H. Kerr, 1992), pp. 18–20. Brian offers a fuller account of his Vietnam experience in *Blood on the Tracks: The Life and Times of S. Brian Willson* (Oakland, CA: PM Press, 2011), chapters 5–7.

Air Force so as to avoid conscription as an infantryman. Arriving in South Vietnam, he was given the job of assessing the effect of U.S. bombing in particular villages. One day,

> [w]hile assessing the "success" of a bombing mission in a small village south of Sa Dec, I looked at the face of a young mother on the ground whose eyes appeared to be open as she held two children in one arm, another child in the other. Upon closer examination I realized she and her children had been killed by bomb fragments.

Tears streamed down Brian's face, he writes. "I looked at that mother's face, what was left of it, and it flashed at that point in my mind that the whole idea of the threat of Communism was ridiculous. . . . I was never to be the same again."

Accompaniment came from an unexpected source. The librarian at the Air Force Base where Brian was stationed had "noticed the books I borrowed, and discerned that I was at odds with other Americans at the Base." She invited Brian Willson to dinner with her family in Can Tho City.

After dinner the family sang songs. One of them, translated into English especially for their guest, concerned a young Quaker named Norman Morrison who had immolated himself at the Pentagon in November 1965 and was a hero to the Vietnamese people. Four of the lines went something like this:

> The flame which burned you will clear and lighten life
> And many new generations of people will find the horizon,
> Then a day will come when the American people
> Will rise, one after another, for life.

Brian suddenly realized that this was the same Norman Morrison who had graduated from Chautauqua High School a few years ahead of him "and had been the first Eagle Scout I ever knew." Again he "broke into tears."

Twenty years later, Brian Willson would sit on a track in California over which trains carried munitions for shipment to Central America, and lose both his legs.

A last example of a man who became a kind of objector while in the military, supported by a kind of accompaniment, is Hugh

Thompson. Thompson exemplifies the way that soldiers, whether conscripts or volunteers, accompany other members of the same small combat unit.

Hugh Thompson was born in Atlanta, moved with his family to nearby Stone Mountain, and in 1965 volunteered for the Warrant Officer Flight Program in the U.S. Army. In Vietnam he commanded a helicopter. The two other crew members were Larry Colburn and Glenn Andreotta, neither of whom had finished high school.[12]

On March 18, 1968, Thompson and his helicopter crew flew a surveillance mission over the hamlet of My Lai. After witnessing more and more appalling scenes, the three men made what Thompson described as a joint decision.

> We did things as a team, normally. Everybody on the aircraft was upset by what we were seeing, and what was going on. We just couldn't explain it. We kept trying to analyze what was happening. And finally reality set in and we said, "You know good and well what's going on down there. Quit fooling yourself!"

Thompson and his crew landed the helicopter, trained their weapons on U.S. troops, and transported two women, five children, and two elderly men to safety. As they flew over the ditch filled with the corpses of men, women, and children, they noticed something moving, landed, and found a girl of five or six, covered in blood and obviously in shock. They flew her to a hospital in Quang Ngai. Years later, Thompson was able to return to Vietnam and greet the child he had saved, now a grown woman.

A Few Practical Considerations

In Iraq and Afghanistan, the volunteer army has been stretched beyond its capacity. I helped to file a lawsuit on behalf of a man from Arkansas who enlisted for service under a contract captioned "Try One." The idea was that he would experience military service for

---

12. For what follows, see Trent Angers, *The Forgotten Hero of My Lai: The Hugh Thompson Story* (Lafayette, LA: Acadian House Publishing, 1999), especially pp. 59–68 (Thompson), 34–36 (Larry Colburn), 39–43 (Glenn Andreotta).

one year and then decide whether he wished to continue. When Mr. Qualls's year was up he told his superiors that he had tried military service for a year and he had decided to go home. He was "Stop Lossed" along with everyone else and ordered to stay in the military. And a federal judge ruled that he should have known that this was a possibility, no matter what his contract said.

To field a military capable of worldwide imperial dominance, the Pentagon finds that it must call forth its volunteers in successive deployments. But these weary volunteers must be given some down time between periods in combat. The objective contradiction between the manpower needs of a volunteer army committed to simultaneous military adventures all over the world, and the human resources required for that project, is likely to express itself between deployments when a soldier is home for so-called R and R.

In the field, the primary emotion has to be solidarity with one's platoon or company, one's fighting unit, in the hope that all may survive. But in down times, the contradiction presents itself. Precisely in those weeks and months, when the things of home again become familiar, when the erstwhile combatant seeks to renew previous relationships, when the faces of children become as real as the faces of comrades in jeopardy, conscientious objection to more of this repellent horror is likely to be most persuasive. Camilo Mejia offers a compelling narrative of that process.[13]

Vietnam left behind a powerful popular memory, just under the surface of daily life. It is as if the soldiers in that ghastly war, dead or alive, still accompany us.

I glimpsed the ineffectiveness of government attempts to suppress the "Vietnam syndrome" when I attended the founding meeting of Labor Against the War early in 2003. The meeting was held at a local union hall of the Teamsters union in Chicago. Teamsters are not well known as opponents of war, so I asked the local union stewards what was going on. They responded, "It was the Vietnam vets. They hit the mike at local union meetings and said that they had seen this movie before."

In Carl Sandburg's *The People, Yes*, a little girl sees her first troop parade. "What are those?" she asks, and is told, "Soldiers." The little girl persists, inquiring, "What are soldiers?" The answer is, "They are

13. Camilo Mejia, *Road from ar Ramadi: The Private Rebellion of Staff Sergeant Camilo Mejia, an Iraq War Memoir* (Chicago: Haymarket Books, 2007).

for war. They fight and each tries to kill as many of the other side as he can." The little girl falls silent. Then she says:

> "Do you know . . . I know something."
> "Yes, what is it you know?"
> "Sometime they'll give a war and nobody will come."[14]

---

14. Carl Sandburg, *The People, Yes* (New York: Harcourt, Brace and Company, 1936), p. 43.

Oscar Romero: An Unlikely Saint

THE PRACTICE THAT CAME TO BE CALLED "ACCOMPANIMENT" WAS widespread among followers of liberation theology in the 1970s and 1980s. Oscar Romero, Archbishop of El Salvador from 1977 until his assassination in 1980, was apparently the first person to use the term.

Does the social origin of a saint matter? Saint Francis of Assisi was the son of a rich merchant. In early adulthood, Saint Vincent de Paul was chaplain to the king of France.

Sometime after the death of his friend Father Rutilio Grande, Monseñor Romero was in Rome accompanied by the Jesuit "provincial" for Central America, Father Cesar Jerez. Jerez remembers:

> We were walking along the Via della Conciliazione. In the distance you could see the dome of the Vatican. It was already late in the evening. . . . I got up my courage to try to get him to speak.
>
> "Monseñor, you've changed. Everything about you has changed. What's happened? . . .Why did you change?"
>
> "You know, Father Jerez, I ask myself that same question when I'm in prayer." He stopped walking and was silent.
>
> "And do you find an answer, Monseñor?"
>
> "Some answers, yes. It's just that we all have our roots, you know. I was born into a poor family. I've suffered hunger. I know what it's like to work from the time you're a little kid. When I went to seminary and started my studies, and then they sent me to finish studying here in Rome, I spent years and years absorbed in my books, and I started to forget about where I came from. I started creating another world. When I went back to El Salvador, they made me the bishop's secretary in San Miguel. I was a parish priest for 23 years there, but I was still buried under paperwork. And when they sent me to San Salvador to be auxiliary bishop, I fell into the hands of [the reactionary movement within the Catholic Church] Opus Dei."

We were walking slowly. It seemed like he wanted to keep talking.

> "Then they sent me to Santiago de Maria, and I ran into extreme poverty again. Those children that were dying because of the water they were drinking, those campesinos killing themselves in the harvests.
>
> "You know, Father, when a piece of charcoal has been lit once, you don't have to blow on it much to get it to flame up again. And everything that happened to us after I got to the archdiocese, what happened to Father Grande and all . . . it was a lot. You know how much I admired him. When I saw Rutilio dead, I thought, 'If they killed him for what he was doing, it's my job to go down that same road.'
>
> "So yes, I changed, but I also came back home again."[1]

So perhaps the social origin of a saint does matter. If the saint has an upper- or middle-class background, acting out the "preferential option for the poor" may resemble an act of charity. Such a person may need to bring a needed professional skill to the table in order to create trusting and mutually respectful relationships with those who are heavy-laden. But if the saint grew up in poverty, as did Monseñor Romero, there may be a more natural opportunity for a relationship of equality with the poor in which each can learn from the other.

Apprenticeship

Oscar Arnulfo Romero was born on August 15, 1917, in the small town of Ciudad Barrios near the border between Honduras and El Salvador. One of Oscar's brothers remembers that the family "scraped by."

> Mother had to rent out the upper part of the house, so the laundry area got moved to the downstairs patio where there was no roof. When it rained everything got soaked. She got wet one too many times working out there and . . . ended up crippled.

---

1. María López Vigil, *Oscar Romero: Memories in Mosaic* (Washington, DC: EPICA, 2000), pp. 158–59.

Their father lost some coffee lands to a moneylender. "So we barely managed to put food on the table for everyone."[2]

When Oscar was thirteen, a young priest came to Ciudad Barrios to offer his first mass. The vicar-general of San Miguel diocese came to Ciudad Barrios for the occasion. Oscar spoke to the vicar-general about his desire to attend seminary. The next year, Oscar left Ciudad Barrios for the seminary in San Miguel, run by the Claretians. In 1937, he went on to the national seminary in San Salvador, run by the Jesuits. After seven months there, his bishop sent him to Rome to complete his studies.

Romero was ordained a priest in April 1942. For a time, he was a parish priest in the mountain town of Anamoros. Then he was called to San Miguel to be secretary of the diocese. He grew famous as a preacher, and at one time five radio stations in this small city simultaneously broadcast his Sunday morning mass. He visited the city jails, where he offered the convicts not only mass but movies to relieve the drabness of their lives. A friend who first met Romero by going to hear his sermons recalls that in his preaching he insisted on a religion that dealt with daily life and not mere piety. "The kingdom of heaven begins right here," he would say.[3]

The new pastoral methods coming into use in those years under the influence of Vatican II and the 1968 gathering of Latin American bishops at Medellín encouraged the training of lay leaders, catechists, and "Delegates of the Word," as well as the formation of base communities among campesinos. Lay catechists as well as priests and religious offered instruction not only before first communion, but also preceding confirmation, marriage, and the baptism of one's children.

As a parish priest, Father Romero was tolerant with habitual drunkards. Poor people such as shoeshine boys were welcome to sleep at the convent. He always had coins in the pocket of his black cassock, and people seeking alms from him would form a line in the early morning. "And if campesinos came in from the countryside, he'd give them bus fare for their return."[4]

There was an area devastated by lava from a volcano where the poorest people lived. When one of those who lived there was close to

---

2. Ibid., p. 17.
3. James R. Brockman, *The Word Remains: A Life of Oscar Romero* (Maryknoll, NY: Orbis Books, 1982), p. 35.
4. López Vigil, *Memories*, p. 26.

death, he or she would ask to confess to Father Romero. "He never told them no."[5]

Romero cultivated relationships with all classes, and when his mother died everyone came to the funeral. "On the way to the cemetery after the funeral Mass, who do you think he walked with? He didn't go with the upper crust, he walked alongside the ones in simple dress, in country clothes—us! 'I was born with them. I'll go with them,' he said quietly."[6]

In 1974, Romero was named bishop of Santiago de Maria. The diocese included his birthplace, Ciudad Barrios, was mostly rural, and numbered more than four hundred thousand.

In 1974 and 1975, Romero was obliged to respond when National Guardsmen and policemen attacked and murdered campesinos in his diocese. Romero protested, but he did so privately. In a letter to his fellow bishops he stated that he did not wish to make a public protest for three reasons: "(1) he thought it better to intervene directly with the authorities; (2) the church was not directly involved with the affair; (3) he was not sure of the real motives behind the killings or of what the conduct of the victims had been." In the words of his biographer, he was a man still believing that the public authorities were not as bad as the actions of their subordinates.[7]

Bishop Romero wrote in the diocesan weekly periodical that "the Church must cry out the command of God [and then, quoting Vatican II, *Gaudium et Spes*]: 'God has meant the earth and all it contains for the use of the whole human race. . . . Whatever the form of property-holding, we must not lose sight of this universal purpose of all wealth.'"[8] But he offered no solution to the injustice of landlords beyond wishing that they were not so selfish and fraudulent.

In mid-1976, Bishop Romero organized a three-day workshop for his clergy on the land reform program announced by the government, which, though small, was concentrated in his diocese. Ruben Zamoro recalled:

> He asked me to give a few talks on the subject. I'll never forget that image: me explaining the agrarian reform to all of

5. Ibid., p. 27.
6. Ibid., p. 32.
7. Brockman, *The Word Remains*, p. 47.
8. Ibid., p. 48.

these priests, with Romero sitting at a student's desk in the front row, taking notes and listening to me super-attentively. The man wanted to learn.[9]

But in October 1976, Salvadoran President Molina, under pressure from the landlords, cancelled even the modest land reform that had been projected.

Juan Macho, a Passionist priest, recalls that Romero told Father Macho and his colleagues at the Los Naranjos Center, "The teaching you do is too participatory." However, in his second year as bishop, according to Father Macho "he started realizing that the campesinos who arrived to work the coffee harvest on the plantations were sleeping on the sidewalks, scattered around the plaza, shivering with cold." One day he asked, "What can be done?" Father Macho suggested using "that big old house where the school used to be." Bishop Romero opened it up and three hundred people could fit inside. In addition, he opened a little classroom that was also used for clergy meetings. Another thirty people could sleep there.

Romero asked the people in Caritas to provide a hot drink at night to these laborers. He "would go around and talk to them. He spent a lot of time listening."[10]

Father Macho is also the source of the following revealing story. One day he told Romero that landowners in the diocese were paying less than the legal minimum wage. Romero could not believe it. "Look," the Passionist replied, you can go to such-and-such a plantation and see it written on a blackboard. Romero went to the plantation to find out.

When he came back he told Father Macho, "You were right, but how is so much injustice possible?" Father Macho replied, "Monseñor, this world so full of injustices is exactly what they were talking about in Medellín." Previously, when Medellín was mentioned, Romero "would get so nervous, he'd develop a tick. The corner of his lip would start trembling, it would shake and shake, and he couldn't control it." But on this occasion, he listened to the word and repeated it to himself: "Medellín. Medellín." And "his lip didn't tremble. After that day, I never saw that tick reappear."[11]

----

9. López Vigil, *Memories*, p. 70.
10. Ibid., 71–72.
11. Ibid., pp. 71–73.

Becoming Archbishop

Clearly, it was events in the first weeks and months following his elevation to Archbishop in February 1977 that caused the well-meaning but cautious church bureaucrat to turn toward martyrdom. Here is a rough chronology:

February 20, 1977. A new president of El Salvador is elected. It was immediately obvious that there had been massive fraud.

February 21, 1977. Romero sends a letter to Salvadoran priests. Aware that most of the clergy were unhappy with his selection as Archbishop, he wrote as follows: "I wish to tell you of the spirit of cooperation that I offer you and that I need from you so that together we can . . . build His church."

February 23, 1977. A private ceremony is held without the usual presence of government representatives to recognize Romero as Archbishop.

February 27, 1977. A huge crowd gathers in Plaza Libertad to protest fraud in the election. Troops open fire on the protesters. Fifteen hundred to three thousand flee to the El Rosario Church on the side of the square. Outgoing Archbishop Chavez and Bishop Rivera negotiate a truce. Romero had gone to his old diocese of Santiago de Maria to wind up his affairs. Ruben Zamora reaches Romero on the telephone and begs him to come to the capital. He cannot extract a promise from the new Archbishop.[12] But Romero did come. A weary Bishop Rivera, his auxiliary bishop, unexpectedly encounters Romero in the early morning hours on the streets of San Salvador. Romero says: "They called me in Santiago at midnight, and here I am."[13]

March 5, 1977. The bishops compose a strong letter drafted by Bishop Rivera. Romero is one of two persons who finalize the draft. The letter states that the church and its priests were being assaulted, but there was a greater sin: the state of suffering in which the majority of Salvadorans live. The mission of the church is to proclaim the kingdom of God, "to struggle for and to further justice, to know the truth, to achieve a political, social, and economic order conformed to God's plan." Therefore, the statement continues, "even at the risk of being misunderstood or persecuted, the church must lift its voice when injustice possesses society."

---

12. López Vigil, *Memories*, pp. 94–96.
13. Brockman, *The Word Remains*, p. 6.

The bishops conclude that the church must be with those for whom no one else shows concern. It "cannot remain unmoved before those who have great tracts of land and those who do not have enough [land] for subsistence."[14] This letter represents one of the last times that the bishops of El Salvador were able to act together during the three years that Oscar Romero was Archbishop.

March 12, 1977. Romero arrives unexpectedly at a parish meeting in which Bishop Rivera is taking part. The Bishops' letter was to be read in masses the next day. Romero has had second thoughts about the statement. "It was untimely, it was partial, he didn't know why it had been issued." He agrees to read it at the 8 a.m. mass but not at a later mass for an audience of more wealthy and powerful people at San José de la Montaña.[15]

That same day, Father Rutilio Grande is murdered.

Rutilio Grande

Rutilio Grande was one among many priests who took part in the new work of the Church in El Salvador. Grande had lived until he was twelve in the hamlet of El Paisnal, which is part of Aguilares, and the destination to which he was driving when he was murdered. He became a Jesuit. Later, he was prefect of discipline at a seminary where he met Romero.

When Romero became a bishop in 1970, he asked Grande to be master of ceremonies at the ordination. In 1971 Grande went to Quito, Ecuador, and took a course at the Instituto Pastoral in which he observed methods of pastoral work that he would use in El Salvador. In 1972, Grande became pastor of Aguilares. There were thirty thousand campesinos in Aguilares. Most of the flat land in the area was held in thirty-five haciendas and grew sugar cane. In El Salvador as a whole, 40.9 percent of rural families were landless in 1975.

In Aguilares, Grande worked with a team of younger Jesuits. They set in motion a process of electing catechists, so-called "Delegates of the Word." From September 1972 to January 1973 the team worked in the town of Aguilares, and from January to June 1973 in the surrounding countryside. The area was divided into a number of districts.

---

14. Ibid., p. 7.
15. Ibid., p. 8

The team gave two-week "missions" district by district. During the mission the team would live in the area, each member deliberately eating each meal at a different house, making the utmost effort to meet all the people. As a matter of principle, they had decided not to accept hospitality from landlords.

In evening sessions to which the whole community was invited, a Scripture passage was read at least twice and by different readers. The idea was to work within the framework of people's religious vision, but to deepen that traditional vision and to transform it from an attitude of passivity to an active struggle for change. After the scripture reading the attendees broke up into groups of eight or ten for discussion.

Toward the end of the two-week period, a number of natural leaders would begin to emerge and Delegates of the Word were chosen by all present. "The emphasis was on a spirit of service and on a collective leadership, and there was an average of one Delegate for every four or five participants. As the mission closed, the Delegates were presented to the community in a formal manner and baptisms were celebrated."[16]

What did Rutilio Grande believe? A number of his addresses and sermons have survived. In them he made several points:

1. The Church should have nothing to do with political groups of any kind. The only politics would be announcement of the Gospel.
2. All injustices would be denounced whatever their source.
3. The goal was "a community of brothers and sisters, committed to building a new world, with no oppression or oppressed, according to God's plan."
4. There would be no sharp division between those within the Christian community and those outside it.

Jon Sobrino recalls that in August 1970, on the occasion of the Feast of the Transfiguration, Father Grande, at the time a candidate for appointment as rector of the seminary, had been the homilist at a solemn mass attended by all the bishops as well as government officials and the diplomatic corps. Grande spoke about the three words inscribed on the Salvadoran flag, "God, Unity, Freedom." He said that because unity and freedom were absent

16. Phillip Berryman, *The Religious Roots of Rebellion: Christians in Central American Revolutions* (Maryknoll, NY: Orbis Books, 1984), pp. 107–8.

in El Salvador, God could not be present, either. He was not appointed rector.[17]

On February 13, 1977, Grande preached what may have been the sermon that caused his assassination. He said in part:

> We all have a common Father. So we are all obviously brothers and sisters.
>
> God the Lord in his plan gave us the material world for everyone without limits. That's what Genesis says, not what I say.
>
> So the material world is for all without limits. It's a common table with a large tablecloth like the Eucharist. And so everyone will come up to it, a tablecloth and food for all. Christ had a reason for making a supper the sign of his kingdom.

Father Grande also said in this sermon:

> Some people cross themselves in the name of the father (money), and the son (coffee) and the spirit (especially if it's cane liquor). That's not the God who is the Father of our Brother and Lord, Jesus, who gives us the good Spirit so that we can all be sisters and brothers in equality, and so that we, the faithful followers of Jesus, can work to make his Reign present here among us.

"It's practically illegal to be a true Christian in our country," Grande continued.

> The mere proclamation of the Gospel is subversive. I'm very afraid that soon the Bible and the Gospel won't be able to enter our borders. We'll just get the bindings because all the pages are subversive.

Grande went on to say that the State wishes to encourage "a false God, in the clouds, sitting on a hammock."

---

17. Jon Sobrino, *Archbishop Romero: Memories and Reflection* (Maryknoll, NY: Orbis Books, 1990), p. 4.

I'm afraid that if Jesus of Nazareth came back, coming down from Galilee to Judea, that is from Chichicastenango to San Salvador, I daresay he would not get as far as Apopa. They would stop him in Guazapa and jail him there.[18]

The organizing and sermonizing found a response among the poor of Aguilares. Ernestina Rivera was a "rezadora," who, in addition to selling food, was called on to say prayers for the dead, which she did without charging any money. The Jesuit team went to her home and found only her children. The priests asked, Is your mother "one of those fireworks types?" The children did not understand, and when Señora Rivera finally met Father Grande, she asked him what he meant.

Grande replied, "Fireworks Christians are the ones that only look upward like the fireworks we light on our feast days. . . . They don't concern themselves with their neighbors."[19]

Apolinario Serrano, nicknamed "Polin," came to be regarded as perhaps the most formidable campesino organizer in the country. One day he was heard to complain, "Oh my God! My head is *this big*! I can't fit anything else in it!" Polin decided that he must learn to read and write so as to have room in his head for all the new things he was learning. Polin had cut sugar cane since childhood, and had fingers deformed from that work. He became a Delegate of the Word and, a friend remembered, "everyone in Aguilares understood the words that came out of his mouth."[20]

From their first meeting, Polin and Archbishop Romero became friends. Romero asked Polin why he was regarded as someone who was inciting the campesinos but was also a man of faith. Polin said it was because he asked questions. He asked Romero if he knew how much a campesino was paid for a day of backbreaking work. The Archbishop wasn't sure. Polin said it was three colones, although "it probably costs more to have your cassock washed."[21]

Constant tension developed between, on the one hand, the work of Grande and teams like the one in Aguilares, and on the other hand, the more political "popular organizations" that formed during those same years. Should the Jesuits limit themselves to

---

18. Berryman, *Roots of Rebellion*, pp. 119–21; López Vigil, *Memories*, pp. 89–90.
19. López Vigil, *Memories*, pp. 86–88.
20. Ibid., pp. 88–89.
21. Ibid., p. 136.

"conscientizacion," or as we might say in the States, consciousness-raising? Or did the notion of "staying with the people" mean that priests and sisters should work closely with the popular organizations or even join such groups?

Father Grande said about violence, "We have not come with the sword, or the machete. Our work is not that. Our violence is in the Word of God, the Word that forces us to change ourselves so that we can make this world a better place."[22]

It may be that a sense that he and his colleagues were losing out to those who advocated guerrilla war caused Grande to feel that he was failing. Grande himself described this dilemma as a "Galilean crisis" for himself and his team. The term evidently referred to the belief of some Biblical scholars that Jesus, carrying out his ministry in the Galilee, saw his popularity diminish and opposition grow.[23]

On the other hand, a resident of an outlying canton recorded these memories:

> The priests of Aguilares came to our canton on March 23, 1975. Before the mission, the place was a mess. . . . But after the mission [there was] no more drunken, disorderly behavior. It used to be that everyone did their own thing. Now we have collective projects. . . . The feuds that we had between the different family groups—all of that has changed now. The people received the mission with open arms. And after it ended, we were left with a whole bunch of trained Delegates of the Word, about thirty of them. You could see the excitement in people.[24]

One old man was asked if he remembered Father Grande. "Sure, I remember him," was the reply. "And what do you remember most about him?" "What I remember about him most of all is that one day he asked me what I thought. No one had ever asked me that in all of my seventy years."[25]

These words reflect the deep influence on the work in Aguilares and elsewhere of the Brazilian educator Paolo Freire. One participant

---

22. Ibid., pp. 89–90.
23. Berryman, *Roots of Rebellion*, pp. 114–15.
24. López Vigil, *Memories*, pp. 90–91.
25. Ibid., p. 91.

recalls, "We would apply Freire's literacy model to our evangelization campaigns so that whatever change was to come would come from the campesinos themselves." María López Vigil explains that Freire's "teaching model emphasizes that the poor already have immense knowledge that stems from their own experience. A teacher's job is to help students share and analyze experiences, and to offer some technical input, such as literary skills, to help them move toward their own liberation."[26]

Responding to Father Grande's Murder

Father Grande's assassination was the first murder of a priest in modern El Salvador.

Romero arrived in Aguilares about 10 p.m. He conferred with the provincial superior of the Jesuits, Cesar Jerez. The bodies of Grande and the two persons killed with him (an old man and a boy) were laid out on tables, covered with sheets. At about 3 a.m. practitioners arrived to perform a preliminary "autopsy" but because of their poor instruments were unable to extract a single bullet.

At 4 a.m. Romero gave instructions to prepare a mass, that night, then and there. Romero asked Father Marcelino Perez what the reading would be. He was told, the Gospel of John, 15:13: "Greater love hath no man than this, that a man lay down his life for his friends." He asked about the additional readings and was told, "That's already done. . . . The three of them are the first reading." Fifteen priests concelebrated.[27]

After the mass, the Archbishop asked clergy and sisters to stay. Campesinos stayed, too. And, Sobrino remembers, "we held a planning session right then and there, in the late hours of the night, without waiting for the next day or a night's rest."

The next day Romero read the bishops' controversial letter, which he had previously decided to read only at the early morning mass, at *both* his masses, including that in San José de la Montaña. In his commentary, he addressed the audience as "those of us who remain on pilgrimage." He said that the Church offers a message of faith: without faith, "all will be feeble, revolutionary, passing, violent." The liberation that Grande preached was based on faith, Romero said. He

---

26. Ibid., p. 92n.
27 Ibid., pp. 105–6.

thanked Grande and his two companions as "co-workers in Christian liberation."[28]

That same day Romero wrote to President Molina, repeating his request for an investigation of the murders. A doctor who examined the bodies had said that the wounds appeared to be caused by a type of rifle used by the police. The Church, Romero wrote, would not participate in any official act of the government until convinced that the government was doing everything it could to identify the murderers.

A meeting of archdiocesan clergy was held the following day. Those assembled were broken up into small groups to discuss four questions Romero put to them. Romero made it clear that the discussion was advisory. He would make final decisions.

Discussion focused on two proposed steps:

1. Closing the Catholic schools for several days. The closure was not to be a vacation: the students and their families would be given a questionnaire to fill out, there would be some sort of reading. The governing board of the Catholic schools had been closely divided. However, the clergy overwhelmingly supported the idea. Only six voted no and seven abstained.

2. A single mass to be broadcast throughout El Salvador from the cathedral in the capital. In the morning, there were eighty-four in favor and eighty-two opposed. In the afternoon, there was a large majority in favor.

The meeting also ratified Romero's decision that the Church should not seem to show support for the government by attending official functions until the situation was resolved.

It became clear that a single mass would be opposed by both the papal nuncio and the civil authorities. Romero thereupon called together "unending meetings. . . . There were huge assemblies, lasting eight or more hours, with people present from both the left and the right."[29]

After the last meeting, several of the more radical clergy talked things over. All agreed, "The man has changed." Suddenly, Romero himself headed toward them. Without preliminaries, he said to

---

28. Brockman, *The Word Remains*, pp. 9–10.
29. López Vigil, *Memories*, pp. 111–12; Sobrino, *Memories and Reflections*, pp. 14–15.

them, "Tell me. Tell me, all of you. What should I do to be a good bishop?"

One of those present responded mischievously, "It's easy. Instead of spending six days a week talking to rich old ladies in San Salvador, you should spend six days a week talking to campesinos and one day here."

Romero replied, "That sounds good to me. But I don't know all of the places in the countryside yet where I should go. Why don't you make me a little schedule for those six days."[30]

One of the most affecting stories about Monseñor Romero concerns the afternoon of March 19, the day before the scheduled single mass. A priest named Inocencio Alas, nicknamed "Chencho," was at the archdiocesan offices, helping to prepare 136 signs so that each parish in the archdiocese would have one to carry. We should imagine him on his knees, painting.

The papal nuncio, Archbishop Gerada, appeared. He had a letter for Archbishop Romero and asked where Romero was. Romero was in El Paisnal, conducting a mass at the Festival of San José that Father Grande had intended to celebrate with his people. The nuncio said angrily that Romero should have been at the archdiocesan offices and was about to make a "big mistake" that would cause "a terrible day for the Church." The nuncio gave Chencho the letter for Romero and left.

Romero returned at about 5 p.m. Chencho gave him the letter and Romero went to his office to read it. He came back, very upset, and asked Chencho to read the letter. The letter ordered Romero to cancel the single mass.

"What can I do, Chencho?" Romero asked.

Chencho reminded him that he and only he was responsible to God for decisions in the archdiocese. Romero "looked [at his friend], still searching."

Then Chencho remembered that, fifteen years before, he and Romero had both been involved in the Christian Cursillo Movement. He asked the Archbishop, "Do you remember how we said back then that when we couldn't find the answer to a problem we were facing, the best thing to do was to go and talk with Jesus? Why don't you do that?"

Archbishop Romero went off toward the chapel while Chencho continued to paint the signs. Chencho recalled:

---

30. López Vigil, *Memories*, pp. 112–13.

About an hour later, I saw him coming down that long hallway. He was moving ever so slowly. . . . When he finally stood next to me, I stayed on my knees, painting, trying to pretend I wasn't feeling that tension. . . .

"So, did you have a chance to talk?" I stood up with a can of green paint in my hand.

"Yes, Chencho. We've talked. He's in agreement too."[31]

The next day, more than a hundred thousand people filled the plaza and side streets to hear the mass, which was also broadcast throughout El Salvador. Chencho was one of many priests from all over the country who found a way to be present and went out among the people.

As the Mass began, I noticed that Monseñor Romero was sweating, pale and nervous. And when he began the homily, it seemed slow to me, without his usual eloquence, as if he was reluctant to go through the door of history that God was opening up for him. But after about five minutes, I felt the Holy Spirit descend upon him.

" . . . I want to give public thanks today, here in front of the archdiocese, for the unified support that is being expressed for the only Gospel and for these our beloved priests. Many of them are in danger, and like Father Grande, they are risking even the maximum sacrifice. . . ."

Hearing the name of Rutilio, thousands exploded into applause. As Chencho experienced the moment, "It was then that he crossed the threshold. He went through the door. Because, you know, there is baptism by water, and there is baptism by blood. But there is also baptism by the people."[32]

Testimony of a Witness: Jon Sobrino

Father Sobrino says that his first "personal encounter" with Monseñor Romero was on the evening of March 12, 1977, the day that Father Grande and his companions were murdered.

---

31. Ibid., pp. 115–17.
32. Ibid., pp. 117–18.

Sobrino was among those who waited for the Archbishop and Auxiliary Bishop Rivera at the Jesuit house in Aguilares. The prelates were late, and as night began to fall, the people began to be uneasy. Father Jerez, Provincial of the Jesuits of Central America, decided that the eucharist should begin without Romero and Rivera and all present except Sobrino (he no longer remembers the reason) began to move toward the church.

Suddenly there was a knock. There stood Romero and Rivera. Sobrino, he tells us in his *Memories and Reflections*, was "struck by the serious, preoccupied face" of the Archbishop. They hardly spoke but Romero's demeanor attracted Father Sobrino and overwhelmed him "with the idea that I must somehow help him."

After the mass Romero asked those present to stay. Both clergy and campesinos were part of the discussion. He asked for help from people "whom a few weeks before he had regarded as suspect, as Marxist!" Sobrino comments that the Archbishop was fifty-nine years old, an age at which previous commitments "typically harden." Moreover, while Romero had considered Father Grande a close friend, he had not approved of Grande's pastoral mission in Aguilares: it seemed to him too political, too "horizontal," foreign to the basic mission of the Church, and dangerously close to revolutionary ideas. Father Sobrino believes that on the night of his friend's murder, Romero, as he looked at the bodies, decided that Grande had been right and he, Romero, had been wrong.

The reactions of conservative people and entities in the Church hierarchy also played a part, Sobrino believes. He remembers Romero at the archdiocesan radio station showing him a letter, written on elaborate stationery, deploring the apparent radicalizing of Romero's outlook. Romero's comment to Sobrino was two words: "Opus Dei."

The day after the single mass of March 20 there was another difficult face-to-face meeting with the nuncio.

Romero decided to go to Rome. Paul VI spoke with Romero privately. Romero gave him a photograph of Rutilio Grande and explained what he was trying to do. The Pope took both of Romero's hands in his and said, "Coraggio!" ("Have courage!").[33]

---

33. Brockman, *The Word Remains*, p. 20.

Words and a Procession

According to St. John, words matter. Here are some of the words spoken by and to Romero after Father Grande's death.

In May, two months after the murder of Father Grande, military forces overran the parish of Aguilares. About five hundred campesinos had long rented land on the Hacienda San Francisco in El Paisnal. They asked for lower rent so that they could afford to plant their corn. The owner told them to leave but the peasants had nowhere to live or to farm, and so "occupied" the land. Father Marcelino accompanied them. The Archbishop went to talk with the landlord, but she would not budge. She then went to see the president.

Two thousand troops with armored cars surrounded Aguilares in the early morning dark. There was an exchange of fire. The military shot and killed a boy named Miguel as he rang the church bells in warning.[34] They carried off three Jesuits and expelled them from the country. Many campesinos were killed or dragged away.

On June 19, 1977, Archbishop Romero went to Aguilares to speak at the installation of new clergy there. The base communities of San Salvador organized a trip to accompany him. Ten priests, including Father Sobrino, concelebrated. Romero thanked the Oblate Sisters who had taken on the work in Aguilares because it was felt to be too dangerous for any priest.

Romero said in part, "It has become my job to tend to all the wounds produced by the persecution of the Church, to record the abuses and pick up the bodies dumped along the side of the road. Today it is my job to tend . . . above all, these people who have been humiliated and sacrificed in such an inhuman way." Sobrino understood this as a description of Romero's "celebrated ministry of accompaniment."

The first reading of the day (Zech. 12:10–11) spoke of the mourning for one who was pierced through. In his homily, Romero denounced those who "have transformed a people into a prison and a torture chamber."

The parish had been a model and leader of the new pastoral concepts, the Archbishop continued. Now it was also the leader in being persecuted. Romero told the afflicted campesinos: "We suffer with

---

34. López Vigil, *Memories*, pp. 167–69.

those who have suffered so much. . . . We suffer with the lost, those who have had to run away and who do not know what is happening to their families. . . . We are with those who are being tortured." At the end, the five thousand people present applauded a message that many would remember for years.

After the mass, Romero invited those attending to join him in procession through the streets, carrying the Blessed Sacrament. According to Sobrino, it was to purify the places that the National Guard had profaned.

Hundreds of people circled the little square at the front of the church, singing and praying. Across the square, in front of the town hall, soldiers stood watching, "sullen, arrogant, and unfriendly." As the procession neared, Sobrino says, "several of them went to the middle of the road and pointed their rifles at us. . . . Those at the front [of the procession] stopped and gradually so did those further back. . . . There we were, face to face with the rifles." In fact, Sobrino confesses, "we were afraid."

All turned instinctively to Romero, who was walking at the rear carrying the monstrance (the receptacle in which the consecrated host is exposed for adoration). He said in a loud voice,

"Adelante!" (Forward!). "Then, little by little, we moved toward the soldiers, and little by little they began to back up. We moved forward. They moved backward. . . . Finally they lowered their rifles and let us pass." The procession ended without incident.[35]

The new president of El Salvador, General Carlos Romero, was to be inaugurated on July 1. Traditionally, Salvadoran bishops attended the ceremony as guests of the government. As he had done repeatedly and would continue to do, Archbishop Romero sought the counsel of colleagues. Of thirteen members of the priests' senate of the diocese, only one favored Romero attending and eleven voted against it. The nuncio thought he should attend. The bishops were divided.

The Archbishop did not attend. But as he explained on the radio, "this does not mean a declaration of war or a definitive break." Quoting from his homily the previous Sunday, Romero added, "Peace is a product of justice [but even] justice is not enough, love is also necessary. The love that makes us feel that we are brothers and sisters is what makes for true peace. . . . Peace is thus the product of justice and love."[36]

---

35. Ibid., pp. 170–71.
36. Brockman, *The Word Remains*, pp. 59–60.

On July 16, 1977, Romero preached in Santa Tecla. He said in part, "When the Church demands a more just society, wealth better shared, more respect for human rights, the Church is not meddling in politics or becoming Marxist and Communist. The Church is telling people [that] only those will be saved who can use the things of earth with the heart of God."[37]

Meantime, as Archbishop Romero labored to explain himself to the people, messages from the people poured in to him. Among them:

"I never felt the church was so close to us poor people";

"I feel happy when you speak only the truth";

"Your homilies and talks move us to continue stronger and more forceful in this struggle to build a more just order and beginning first with ourselves";

"We are one with you and very happy to have a good shepherd and prophet of our time";

"We greet you in the name of this community, and not only this, but at the same time we inform you that we totally agree with your consideration in the present situation, which horrifies the whole country, and especially the Church, which is the bearer of the message of truth, the way and the life";

"We'll continue our struggle until we succeed in building the kingdom of God on earth";

"As you are ready to give your lives for Jesus Christ so are we";

"Without any fear we will keep on preaching in the light of the gospel the good news to the poor";

"The more we are threatened the braver we feel and therefore we write you not to feel alone, we are all ready to accept any sacrifice."

In the words of biographer James Brockman, "Many letters were signed with a collection of thumbprints. It is not hard to visualize a group of wiry, weatherbeaten men and women gathered around the light of a candle while the one or two literate members traced the words on a tablet for all to sign and one to take over the mountain paths to a distant small-town post office."[38]

---

37. Ibid., pp. 65–66.
38. Ibid., pp. 67–69.

Life with the Least of These

Anecdotes abound as to how Monseñor Romero lived out, day by day, the instruction of Matthew 25 about living with "the least of these."

Monseñor visited a canton for the festival of St. Anthony. Because the crowd was so large, he held mass under a tree. Afterward, a line formed to wish him goodbye.

An old woman was last in line. "When he hugged me, he said, 'Pray for me.' He wanted *me*, an old sinful woman, to pray for him! How many times does that happen? From that day on, I always prayed for him."[39]

Another old woman, from Chaletenango, went to his office in San Salvador. Romero was not there and was anxiously awaited by all the bishops for a meeting. Finally he arrived.

Romero noticed the little old woman sitting on a bench. "And you?" he asked, "Have you been helped?" Apparently a family member had disappeared.

He put his arm around her shoulder and they began to walk up and down the corridor.

"Monseñor, the bishops are waiting for you!" the secretary reminded him with more urgency in her voice.

"Well, tell them I'd like them to wait or come back tomorrow. But I'm not going to make this woman wait for me."

A half hour later, the two of them were still talking.[40]

The archdiocesan office became a sea of people. The campesinos arrived with hens, roosters, and one day, even a cow! The office workers approached Monseñor about setting up a more firm schedule of appointments. He asked them exactly how it would work. They explained. He responded, "I don't think that kind of scheduling is going to be possible."

"No?"

"No, because I have my priorities. I'm always going to receive any campesino that shows up here at any time of day, whether I'm in a meeting or not. . . . Look, my fellow bishops all have cars. The parish priests can take buses, and

39. López Vigil, *Memories*, pp. 146–47.
40. Ibid., p. 175.

they can afford to wait. But what about the campesinos? They come walking for miles, face all kinds of dangers, and sometimes they haven't eaten. . . ."

I started crumpling up the papers I'd prepared on which I'd written a scheduling proposal for him.

"You know [he added,] the campesinos never ask me for anything. They just talk to me about the things that are going on in their lives."[41]

In all phases of his service in the Church, Monseñor Romero resisted fancy accommodations and expensive gifts. When he first became Archbishop, he slept in the sacristy right behind the back wall of the chapel at a cancer hospital managed by an order of Sisters. They decided to build him a little house.

"It will be a very simple house, Monseñor."

"It better be, or I'm leaving."

One little living room, a bath and two bedrooms, "in case you have any guests."

"No, what I want there is a hammock."[42]

As campesinos and their families joined the popular organizations, repression grew. And the more blood flowed, the more people joined the organizations. One day campesinos took over the parish house in Aguilares.

I went rushing off to San Salvador to find Monseñor Romero.

"Is there a danger of a massacre?" he asked me.

"When isn't there? What do you think we priests and nuns should do?"

"What the campesinos are doing is just, and you should always be at their side.

Accompany them. Take the same risks they do."[43]

Another memory:

---

41. Ibid., pp. 148–49.
42. Ibid., p. 152.
43. Ibid., p. 248.

On holidays they gave us seminarians some time off. There were about six of us older students who decided that May 1st to go to the union march. That evening the directors of the seminary called us in. "You want to be involved in politics? Well then, you'll have to leave the seminary."

The team informed Monseñor Romero, and the next day he called us in to talk with him. He began to tell us about the report he'd received about us. He had it there in his hands. He looked so serious that we started to get worried.

"Look," he said to us solemnly, "you're in seminary to learn, and you have to learn to obey, to sacrifice and respect authority."

He paused, and we knew the six of us would be kicked out.

"But, you also to have learn about the realities of the people, because you come from the people, and you came here to learn how to serve the people. So . . . don't worry. You're staying. If they throw you out, they'd have to throw me out, too!"[44]

And another:

I had to go into hiding. My bishop excommunicated me and suspended me [from performing priestly functions]. I found a place in San Salvador. I'd celebrate mass in people's homes. We used to call it "catacomb ministry."

Mother Teresita provided us space in some corner of the cancer hospital for those meetings. But Monseñor Romero didn't know about them. One day [she said to me]: "if there's nothing wrong in what you're doing, why are you doing it behind Monseñor Romero's back?"

She was right. I told him everything [and he said]: "You have my support, son. But tell me, where are you living?"

"I live where I can. I have to keep moving around. I don't have a fixed place to lay my head."

"Well, you've always got a place here."

So on many a night I went to sleep in the guest room in his house. He liked me to visit so I could talk to him about what I was doing.

44. Ibid., pp. 253–56.

"I've even had to celebrate Mass with coffee and semita bread."

"Hey, but those Masses don't count!" he said.

"They're being celebrated by communities of people who are all ready to give their lives for each other. Doesn't that count?"[45]

And then, a young priest who may very well have joined the guerrillas, and carried a weapon, was murdered. The question was whether Romero should attend the funeral. Monseñor called eight priests to have dinner with him. He said,

> "In order to make the decision I need to make, I'm just asking myself one question right now."
>
> We, who had arrived trembling, were even more frightened now. What would he ask us? If Neto had or hadn't joined the guerrillas? If he carried a weapon or not?
>
> "What I'm asking myself is this. What must Doña Marita, Neto's mother, be thinking now? Would it matter to her if Neto was carrying a weapon or not? If he was a guerrilla or not? Neto was her son, and she was his mother. The Church is also Neto's mother, and as a bishop I am his father. I should be by his side as well."
>
> He looked at each of us, one by one. "You have to be at his side too. We're going to say good-bye to him with a Mass, like the priest that he is. Come, let's go get things ready."[46]

And:

> Of course we remembered the argument we'd had with Monseñor Romero in Zacamil in 1972. Six years later, Monseñor was there with us again in the same place. But this time it was a welcome party we'd invited him to. We had cake, songs, streamers. No one was going to mention the problem we'd had with him years ago.

---

45. Ibid., pp. 257–59.
46. Ibid., pp. 262–64.

No one but him, that is. He brought it up as soon as he got there. We couldn't speak. The guy who was running the record player decided to turn it off, and the person opening soda bottles dropped one on the floor and it broke. Monseñor said: "I was wrong, and you were right. That day you taught me about faith and about the Church. Please forgive me for everything that happened then."

Well, all of us, young and old, started crying.[47]

And also:

[It's a long story, but in the remote canton of La Libertad I met an eight-year-old boy named Emilio with an infected foot that smelled horribly. I asked and received his mother's permission to take him with me to a hospital in San Salvador. When we reached the city he asked me for a favor. I wondered, A bicycle? A trip to the ocean? Emilio said: "I want to meet Monseñor Romero."]

One day in the hospital I saw Monseñor arrive. Emilio saw him too.

"Monseñor," I told him, "what this little guy wants most in life is to meet you."

"Well, let's get acquainted. So what's your name?"

"Emilio Valencia. I'm from El Almendral."

He sat down and put Emilio in his lap.

"Tell me about your canton. I've never been there,"

I can't describe the look of joy on the face of that child.

Emilio had the pleasure of going back home cured. But he lived for only two more years. A few days before Monseñor Romero was killed, the National Guard attacked and burned down his entire canton, killing him and the rest of his family.[48]

One more:

I was in one of the cantons of Aguilares with four campesinos. One of them was the famous Polin.

---

47. Ibid., pp. 267–68.
48. Ibid., pp. 268–70.

"We're going to meet for a while to study the Bible," one said. They had the Bible hidden, buried under the ground in a plastic container.

We'd been at it for more than an hour when way, way off in the distance we saw a little dot moving toward us. It was Monseñor Romero.

"What are you all doing?"

"We're reading the Gospel of John."

"Would you allow a pastor to sit down with you?" he asked them.

"Pull up a chair, Monseñor," Polin said.

He sat down on a patch of grass. And the men went on for another hour with their reflections—reading calmly and speaking calmly, like the campesinos do, thinking things out so that words aren't wasted.

Monseñor Romero didn't open his mouth. When they were through, I turned around and saw that his eyes were brimming with tears.[49]

Truthfully, this is the last:

La Bernal is like a pit of misery in the middle of several middle class neighborhoods. We arrived to work as catechists. We prepared about 30 kids to receive their First Communion on the afternoon of December 24. The kids had the idea: "Why don't we invite Monseñor Romero?"

Well, he came. I still remember what he said when he began his homily: "Today we have moved the pulpit from the Cathedral to the neighborhood of La Bernal so that from this small, poor community we can announce the good news of Christmas to the entire community of El Salvador."

After the Mass and the First Communion, we fixed up two tables really nice. Tamales had been made.

Suddenly a little boy appeared from nowhere. He was tiny, about four years old. Covered with dirt, barefoot, and with a nose full of snot. He came up to Monseñor Romero from behind and pulled on his cassock with his grubby fingers.

---

49. Ibid., pp. 271–72.

"You want some?" Monseñor asked him. The little boy nodded. The kid was filthy. Monseñor picked him up, put him on his lap, and started feeding him from his tamal. He'd eat one bite and give the next bite to the boy. And so the two of them ate tamales together that Christmas eve.[50]

A Church Divided

In February 1978, a year after his installation as Archbishop, Romero received an honorary degree from Georgetown University in the San Salvador Cathedral. Notwithstanding the behind-the-scenes opposition of the apostolic delegate in Washington and the prefect of the Congregation for Catholic Education, as well as the absence from the ceremony of the papal nuncio and a majority of El Salvador's bishops, an overflow crowd made clear that the voiceless of El Salvador had found someone to speak for them.

Shortly afterward, without Romero's knowledge, two to three hundred of El Salvador's priests and nuns wrote to the nuncio, deploring Archbishop Gerada's insensitivity "to the silent sorrow of the oppressed and persecuted peasantry, to the tears of the widows and mothers of the disappeared for political reasons, and to our people's hunger for bread and for truth." They prayed that God would help the nuncio to "hear the cry of a whole people in which Jesus continues to die and rise again each day."

Romero had begun in every homily to list the assaults on religious and lay people during the immediately preceding days. Religious buildings within the jurisdiction of the Archbishop, such as the parish house of San José de la Montaña, were opened to ever-increasing numbers of refugees. Romero defended the popular organizations, but wanted to keep the church autonomous from them at all times.

The bishops hostile to Romero began a campaign to oust him from the seminary. He replied that the archdiocesan offices had functioned for seven years in the seminary, which had ample space, and beside, the seminary property belonged to the archdiocese.

---

50. Ibid., pp. 278–79.

No Justice, No Peace

In a homily on April 30, 1978, Archbishop Romero spoke of judges who do not protect the victims of violence but "sell themselves." He received a letter from the Supreme Court requesting the names of the judges that Romero had in mind.

Twenty-five lawyers offered their services to the Archbishop in preparing a reply. He read it aloud at the end of his homily on Pentecost Sunday, May 14. Since he had not been subjected to legal process, he answered the letter in the court to which it was addressed: the court of public opinion.

Romero's reply listed specific human rights, recognized both by the Salvadoran constitution and by international law, that could not be enforced in the courts of El Salvador. These rights included not only the right of habeas corpus—the right to know where a prisoner is confined and the crime of which he has been accused—but rights like the freedom to form labor unions.

He read rapidly, perhaps nervously, and referred to his readiness "to face trial and prison, even though that would add another injustice." When those present applauded long and warmly, he added, "Thank you for the seal of approval that you have placed on my poor words."

The Supreme Court never replied.

In November 1977, the government adopted a statute called the Law for the Defense of Public Order. Its provisions were very vague and very menacing. Romero explained in his sermons that St. Thomas Aquinas taught that a real law must be both just and for the good of society, otherwise it does not require obedience. The law was repealed in 1979.

Again Romero reported and appealed to Rome, and this time he was specifically invited to appear by Cardinal Sebastiano Baggio, prefect of the Sacred Congregation for the Bishops. Baggio told him that there was a feeling on the part of many that Romero had been converted to a new aggressiveness against established institutions.

Romero responded that, as he saw it, "faithfulness to the gospel brings about the division that Christ announced even among members of the same family." He explained that he wished to separate diplomatic and liturgical functions so as not to appear to be blessing the government.

As had been the case previously the Pope, Paul VI, seemed far more encouraging than the Pope's subordinates. Romero wrote in his diary that the Pope encouraged him to be patient and courageous.

In his Second Pastoral Letter (1977),[51] for which his friend Jon Sobrino wrote a first draft, Romero had said, "to the traditional condemnation of atheistic Marxism, the church now adds in equal measure the condemnation of the capitalist system." And in his only remarks to the bishops' conference in Puebla, Mexico (1979), the Archbishop declared, "our document [must respond] to the unjust distribution of the wealth that God has created for all."

But Romero was equally clear that "one cannot do evil in order to achieve good." He condemned the Left when it took and harmed hostages; when it burned vehicles; when it machine-gunned residences; when it occupied offices and locales set aside for the people, including churches; and when on May 23 the minister of education and his chauffeur were ambushed and killed. According to Sobrino, Romero criticized the popular organizations for "their internal divisions, their eagerness for hegemony over other leftist organizations, and [for the attitude that] only a popular organization could ever render service to the people." He also condemned what he considered a tendency "to manipulate popular piety in the interests of the organization."

The Archbishop published a statement asking that the occupation of churches and foreign embassies be discontinued. The occupations had partially achieved their objectives. To "keep stirring up the country seems out of proportion to the objectives [that have not yet been] achieved." He called for a climate that would permit attention to "the structural problems that are at the root of the growing popular discontent."

The Third Pastoral Letter

Romero's Third Pastoral Letter, issued in August 1978 on the occasion of the Feast of the Transfiguration, was his most important.[52]

It is inaccurate to think of this document as a solitary composition, as it were written in the midnight hours by the light of a candle, and

---

51. Archbishop Oscar Romero, *Voice of the Voiceless: The Four Pastoral Letters and Other Statements* (Maryknoll, NY: Orbis Books, 1985), pp. 63–84.
52. Ibid., pp. 85–113.

encompassed between the four borders of the written page. On the contrary, every word had been repeatedly discussed with lay and clerical advisers; the hostile bishops issued a statement of their own after the Pastoral was made public; and to this there was a response from two of the leading popular organizations, the Farm Workers Union (UTC) and the Christian Federation of Salvadoran Peasants (FECCAS).

Our own much-thumbed copy, festooned with bookmarks, paper clips, underlinings, and yellow "post-its," calls attention to the following passages.

In his Third Pastoral Letter, Archbishop Romero considered the relationship between the church and the popular political organizations that were proliferating in El Salvador. People in the countryside asked Romero,

> Does being a Christian mean one has to join some organization seeking radical changes in our country? How can one be a Christian and accept the demands of the gospel and yet join some organization that neither believes in nor has sympathy with the gospel? How ought a Christian to resolve the conflict between loyalty to the gospel and the demands of an organization when it may not be in accordance with the gospel? What is the relationship between the church and these organizations?[53]

The problem of violence arises spontaneously, the Archbishop wrote. Because of the efforts of popular organizations to obtain their social, political, and economic objectives, violence is often regarded as a suitable means. In a situation where people are the victims of kidnappings, murder, torture, threats, arson, and so on, consciences can lose all sensitivity, and we have to go on repeating, "no to violence, yes to peace."[54]

In his Third and Fourth Pastoral Letters, Archbishop Romero described different kinds of violence. The most acute form in which violence appears in Latin America, he said, is "structural" or "institutionalized violence," in which the socioeconomic and political structures operate to the benefit of a minority with the result that the majority of people are deprived of the necessities of life.[55]

---

53. Ibid., p. 88.
54. Ibid., pp. 105–6.
55. Ibid., pp, 106, 143.

"Arbitrary violence of the State," or "repressive violence" by the state security forces, is used to defend the prevailing socioeconomic and political system, crushing any signs of protest, and preventing the people from having any real chance of self-government.[56] Violence by right wing gangs that is allowed to go unpunished likewise upholds the unjust social order.[57]

"Terrorist violence," described as "the explosive revolutions of despair," produces and provokes useless and unjustifiable bloodshed, abandons society to tensions beyond the control of reason, and disparages any form of dialogue as a means of solving social conflicts.[58]

"Spontaneous violence" is an immediate reaction, not calculated or organized, by groups or individuals when they are violently attacked. But because it is marked by desperation and improvisation, it is not an effective way of securing rights or bringing just solutions to conflicts.[59]

"Legitimate self-defense," Archbishop Romero concludes, seeks to neutralize or bring under control, not necessarily to destroy, an imminent, serious, and unjust threat.[60] Certain conditions are necessary to justify insurrection or self-defense. First, the violence used is proportional to, not greater than, the need. For example, if one can defend oneself with one's fists, it is not permitted to shoot an aggressor. Second, resort to violence is justified only after every possible peaceful means has been tried. And third, the violence used in self defense does not bring on even greater evil in retaliation.[61]

Massacre of the Innocents[62]

With the beginning of Advent 1978, the Church ceased to practice infant confirmation. In the future, only children at least eight years of age might be confirmed and pastors were encouraged to prepare adolescents for the sacrament.

---

56. Ibid., pp. 107, 143–44.
57. Ibid., p. 144.
58. Ibid., p. 107, quoting Pope Paul VI; Ibid., pp. 107, 144.
59. Ibid., p. 107.
60. Ibid., p. 107.
61. Ibid., p. 145.
62. Brockman, *The Word Remains*, pp. 140–43; López Vigil, *Memories,* pp. 282–89.

On January 20, 1979, in El Despertar (which means "The Awakening"), about thirty young men were gathered for a weekend retreat called a "young people's Christian initiation gathering."

The gathering was held in a plain brick building on an unpaved street. At 6 a.m. thirty-four-year-old Father Octavio Ortiz went outside the building apparently to investigate the noise of armed men rushing onto the grounds. He was shot dead. Four young men died of gunshots. The survivors were arrested. The government's communiques, writes Brockman, portrayed guitars as weapons and songbooks as subversive literature.

Monseñor went to the morgue that evening. He said of Octavio's body, "You couldn't tell it was him. His body was completely flattened, his face destroyed."

Monseñor Romero knelt on the ground and held his shattered head.

"It can't be. This isn't him. It's not him."

Tears streamed from Monseñor's face as he held him close.

"They ran over him with a tank and smashed his head, Monseñor."

"I can't believe they could be so savage," he said.

The guardsmen looked in through the door. Monseñor's cassock was covered with blood and he was cradling Father Octavio in his arms.

"Octavio, my son, you have completed your mission. You were faithful."

He stayed on the floor without moving, just holding Octavio and looking at him.

The next day, over one hundred priests gathered to concelebrate the Archbishop's regular morning mass. The altar was set up outside the front door of the Cathedral. The Archbishop asked and received permission from the ten to fifteen thousand in attendance to leave the next day to attend the meeting of Latin American bishops in Puebla, Mexico.

He spoke of the life of Octavio Ortiz, born of campesino parents in a village not far from Romero's birthplace. Ortiz was the first priest Romero had ordained. The Archbishop said that he was happy to say that the Church was receiving more applications than ever from young men wishing to become priests.

After a pause, he continued firmly that the president of the country had said that there was no persecution of the Church. "But here in the Cathedral, we see the proof that he is a liar!" The Church, he concluded, defends the image of God in man. There was no conflict between the Church and the government. The conflict was between the government and the people. And "the Church is with the people and the people are with the Church, thanks be to God!" The crowd broke into tumultuous applause.

There was a discussion as to where Father Ortiz should be buried. Five members of his family and people from Mejicanos where he had been working took part. Monseñor said, "We would like to have Octavio buried in the Cathedral as a martyr," but that his family may prefer the village cemetery. The people from the base communities broke in. "Octavio was with us in life, and he should stay here with us now!" "Octavio is not dead. He is living with us still!" And so that was what was done.

One last time he sought to speak with the Pope, who was now John Paul II. María López Vigil, editor of the magnificent collection of oral histories which we have quoted so often, herself contributes what Monseñor told her on May 11, 1979, apparently at the Madrid airport, about his interview with the Pope.

> Monseñor Romero had asked for a personal audience with Pope John Paul II from San Salvador, and he had done so in sufficient time to get through the various obstacles of the Church bureaucracy. The Vatican officials said they didn't know anything about his petition. Romero's time in Rome was coming to an end.
>
> As usual, after Mass on Sunday the Pope went down to an immense meeting hall to greet well-wishers who stood in line. Monseñor Romero got up very early so as to be first in line. He took the Pope's hand and did not let go, begging for an audience. It was granted for the next day.
>
> The Archbishop had brought with him carefully selected reports of what was happening in El Salvador. The Pope didn't wish to read them.
>
> In a separate envelope, Monseñor had brought a photograph of Father Ortiz's face, smashed by the tank that ran over it. The Pope waved it away.
>
> "They said he was a guerrilla," Romero said.

"And wasn't he?" the Pontiff responded coldly.

Over and over the Pope said: "You, Mr. Archbishop, should make efforts to have a better relationship with your country's government."[63]

Deposing the Mighty

Violence from both Right and Left continued through June 1979. One of those killed was a forty-year-old priest named Rafael Palacios who had come to Romero to tell him that he feared for his safety.

But in July 1979, there was a successful insurrection in Nicaragua.

In August, the Archbishop issued his Fourth (and last) Pastoral Letter.[64] He said to his Salvadoran audience, "You and I have written this pastoral letter." This final manifesto sets forth more explicitly than ever the belief that government repression against popular organizations is directed "to maintain and increase profit levels."

Turning to what is to be done, the Pastoral describes some of the answers to a survey the Archbishop had distributed to "my beloved priests and . . . basic ecclesiastical communities." The questionnaire asked what people thought of the country and the church, what they thought was the greatest sin, who Jesus Christ was for them, and what they thought about the bishops, the nuncio, and the Archbishop himself. The Pastoral quotes one of the answers verbatim:

> The church has to interpret for, and to accompany, this people as it struggles for freedom; if not, in the course of time it will be marginalized. With or without the church the changes will take place, but by its very nature its duty is to be present in the midst of these changes, which are delineating the kingdom of God.

Romero proposed that there were three kinds of apostolate.

The first was what he called the "mass apostolate," as when he preached to thousands in or near the cathedral or on the radio.

Second there was the "apostolate for basic Christian communities or small groups." "Living in community" should be expected of all Christians. Christianity demands, he wrote, the "forming of community."

---

63. López Vigil, *Memories*, pp. 302–6.
64. Romero, *Voice of the Voiceless*, pp. 114–61.

But the purpose of Christian community is to "spread the kingdom of God." Such a community cannot present itself as a place of peaceful refuge from the world. Rather, it must be as said in the New Testament, a yeast, a salt, and a light. "One cannot imagine that yeast would fulfill its function if it were not within the dough it had to leaven, or if salt were not within the food to which it had to give flavor, or if light were not in the place it had to illuminate."

Finally, there was what Romero described in the last section of this final Pastoral as "the apostolate of following or companionship."[65] According to Phillip Berryman, the Spanish in which Archbishop Romero described this practice was *pastoral de acompañamiento* (pastoral work of accompanying).

Readers were called on to recognize that individuals would make different choices as to how to bring about the kingdom of God. One phrase echoes the Port Huron Statement of the Students for a Democratic Society (SDS) in the United States, referring to "the aspirations of workers and campesinos who want to be treated like free and responsible people called to share in the decisions that affect their lives."

The Archbishop quoted the Puebla declaration to the effect that the Church must be present in the political "area of reality," because Christianity is intended to evangelize "the whole of human life, including the political dimension." Puebla goes on to criticize "those who would restrict the scope of faith to personal or family life . . . as if sin, love, prayer, and pardon had no relevance" in the public arena.

But precisely in this area the believer is challenged to be flexible and tolerant: by exercising discernment before taking action; by being clear and firm about "the criteria and the values of the gospel" while searching "for greater knowledge about more uncertain issues"; by avoiding personal prejudices that might lead one to pressure others to join a group or "to abandon the choices they have made"; by recognizing that commitment and sacrifice "will entail risks, criticisms, and false accusations."

A paragraph in the Fourth Pastoral Letter makes it clear that Archbishop Oscar Romero did not romanticize the poor:

> The Church knows perfectly well that among those who lack material goods there is a great deal of sinfulness. . . . In

---

65. Berryman, *Roots of Rebellion*, p. 340; see also Berryman, *Stubborn Hope: Religion, Politics, and Revolution in Central America* (Maryknoll, NY: Orbis Books, 1994), p. 173.

the name of the preferential option for the poor there can never be justified the machismo, the alcoholism, the failure in family responsibility, the exploitation of one poor person by another, the antagonism among neighbors, and the so many other sins.

And so he ends, viewing this Fourth Pastoral Letter as "the contribution of one local church to the renewal that Vatican II began, and to which Medellín and Puebla gave concrete shape for the church of Latin America."

Almost

In September and October 1979, six months before Archbishop Romero's assassination, El Salvador came heartbreakingly close to a political breakthrough.

On October 13, 1979, President Romero (no relation to Monseñor) fled to Guatemala and a group of young military officers assumed nominal authority. They asked Archbishop Romero to call for calm, and he did so, cautiously, but filled with hope.

From the outset, the popular organizations took the position that it was all a facade, that nothing fundamental had changed or would change. Archbishop Romero, on the other hand, was tormented by the imminence of civil war and kept saying that there were good people in the new governing junta. There were weeks of painful separation between Monseñor and the young men and women whom he had defended.

The Archbishop and the popular organizations differed about the meaning of an agrarian reform announced by the junta. Monseñor wanted to find hope in the announcement. One campesino told him, "They'll say anything, Monseñor! But we can't just trust fancy words or things written on some paper." Another said, "Monseñor, don't believe in these laws. We know it's the same as always. Their laws are like a snake. They only bite people who are barefoot."[66]

Two Sundays later, when more people had died from the repression, and the law was still only on paper, Monseñor mentioned the agrarian reform in his homily. He compared it to a snake. In the end, the oligarchy regained control of the army. One by one members of

---

66. López Vigil, *Memories*, pp. 360–62.

the junta that had begun to initiate reforms felt compelled to resign. But the repression had never stopped, and in January 1980 violence began to grow again. José Obdulio Chacon said, "Of the 250 of us who used to meet with Father Rutilio Grande in those wonderful communities, there are only three of us left."

Romero's last weeks were a prolonged Gethsemane. In his homily on Sunday February 17, the Sunday before Lent and Ash Wednesday, Romero preached on the Beatitudes. He read aloud his letter to U.S. President Jimmy Carter, asking that the United States stop sending arms to the government of El Salvador. When Monseñor finished reading his letter, the Cathedral shook with applause: "We were applauding as if we'd all signed that letter to the gringos."

The Archbishop appears to have expected his assassination. He told an interviewer two weeks before his death, after apologizing lest he seem pretentious, "If they kill me, I shall rise again in the Salvadoran people."

Colonel Garcia, in charge of the armed forces, came to see Monseñor and offered Archbishop Romero military protection. Monseñor responded, "Colonel Garcia, as long as you don't truly protect the people, I can't accept any protection from you."[67]

Late in February, the YSX radio station that Romero used to broadcast his sermons was dynamited and destroyed. Technicians worked frantically with old, secondhand equipment to restore the Archbishop's voice to the people. They patched it together sufficiently for the Archbishop's Sunday homily of March 23, 1980.

On the day before his murder, Romero made the famous personal appeal to National Guardsmen that was probably the proximate cause of his death:

> Brothers, you are part of our own people. You kill your own campesino brothers and sisters. . . . No soldier is obliged to obey an order against the law of God. . . . It is time to recover your consciences. . . . In the name of God, and in the name of this suffering people whose laments rise to heaven each day more tumultuously, I beg you, I ask you, I order you in the name of God: Stop the repression![68]

---

67. Ibid., p. 395.
68. For a slightly different translation, see Berryman, *Roots of Rebellion*, p. 150.

Almost a half minute of applause followed.

It seems that this dramatic challenge to the Powers That Be was something more than a spontaneous or solitary effort. At a mass on January 20, 1980, two months before his death, Romero had read a letter from a group of soldiers who asked that they "not be sent out to repress the people," and was interrupted by applause. López Vigil provides a short interview with the man who persuaded his fellow soldiers to write to the Monseñor. Ramon Moreno told her:

> They sent us to kill people in the countryside—people whose names we didn't know, let alone what they'd done. More likely, they were Christians like us who were hungry, that's all. And we had to go spray them with bullets, burn their little shacks and steal their pigs and chickens.
>
> But our commanders weren't cruel just to the campesinos. They were also cruel to us. They beat us, too. It really doesn't matter if you're dressed up like a soldier. If you're poor, you're poor.
>
> "Maybe Monseñor Romero will speak up for us. He looks out for poor people," I said one day to a few of the rank and file who were disgruntled with the lives we had to live.
>
> I had gotten the idea from listening to his homilies. And that's why we wrote him that letter he ended up reading one Sunday. We risked our hides by sending it, and he risked his by reading it.[69]

And Phillip Berryman reports, in his book *The Religious Roots of Rebellion*, that the whole March 23 sermon in which Romero appealed to the Guardsmen to stop the repression "had been prepared the day before with a team of priests, sisters, and lay people who normally met for this purpose."[70]

On March 24, the gospel reading for the homily at the chapel adjacent to the cancer hospital was from John 12:23–26: "Unless the grain of wheat falls to the earth and dies, it remains only a grain. But if it dies, it bears much fruit." Or as Archbishop Romero explained

---

69. López Vigil, *Memories*, p. 367.
70. Berryman, *Roots of Rebellion*, p. 150.

the passage, "whoever out of the love for Christ gives himself to the service of others will live, like the grain of wheat that dies, but only apparently dies. If it did not die, it would remain alone."

When the Poor Come to Believe in the Poor

The effort to retrieve and integrate what Romero bequeathed to us has focused on his words. Yet despite all this understandable attention to what Monseñor Romero wrote and said, his greatest contribution lies in what he did, and especially in his style of interaction with the poor.

One finds hints of a reorientation in the words themselves. Over and over again, Archbishop Romero referred to the "preferential option for the poor" set forth in the Medellín and Puebla documents. But that "option" is, self-evidently, a choice made by Church personnel and middle-class intellectuals who may *not* be poor to take up a new way of life in the midst of the poverty surrounding them. The "accompaniment" to which he became committed is something different, more equal, more in the nature of a joint undertaking.

A new vocabulary had to make its way in the face of the assumption embodied in the word "evangelization," namely, that those who opted for the poor had the responsibility of bringing them a message.

This core meaning of "evangelization" had to give way, and did give way, to the idea of the man or woman who brought a message to the poor also receiving a message *from them*; to an emphasis on *listening* rather than talking; and to an ultimate vision of *the poor themselves* taking responsibility for their own liberation.

Thus to the extent the word "evangelization" continued to be used in describing what the Romero Church practiced, it was understood "not as the traditional imparting of doctrine but a two-way dialogue in which the poor expressed their own experience."[71]

Romero's practice of accompaniment was many-sided. For example, Sobrino recalls, "In his visits to parishes, he stood in line, plate in hand, to receive his food just like everyone else."

Romero set up a diocesan cafeteria near his offices where poor people and religious might sit and drink together, and come to know each other better. Groups of peasants and other poor people were always arriving to recount their experiences.

---

71. Ibid., p. 332.

From the first days of his episcopate, the Archbishop sought to make church buildings available to refugees. He suspended his first pastoral meeting, in the midst of the 1977 election crisis, suggesting that the priests return and be ready to receive in their homes those who may be fleeing for their lives. By March 16, 1980, eight days before his death, the two refugee centers that Romero had set up were housing 189 refugees from the countryside, of whom 56 were children under ten years of age. During the next week, two more refugee centers were created.

The new pastoral practice of accompaniment, rather than (in its more traditional sense) evangelization, also makes itself known in some of the Archbishop's last and most formal declarations. At the University of Louvain he said, "It is the poor who tell us what the world is, and what the Church's service to the world should be." The hope that our Church encourages, he went on, is

> a summons from the word of God, for the great majority of the people, the poor, that they assume their proper responsibility, that they *undertake their own conscientizacion. . . .* The hope that we preach to the poor is intended *to give them back their dignity, to encourage them to take charge of their own future.*[72]

Liberation, Romero continued, will arrive only when the poor are not simply on the receiving end of handouts from governments or from the church, but when they themselves are the masters of, and the protagonists in, their own struggle and liberation, thereby unmasking the root of false paternalism, including ecclesiastical paternalism.

In the last sentence of this very nearly last oration to the world, on February 2, 1980, Archbishop Oscar Romero said that what he and his colleagues sought to do was to "put themselves alongside the poor."[73]

Fragments from Monseñor Romero's last conversations are remarkably radical. All through his last weeks, he was having long, mutually respectful conversations with young men and women who had chosen the path of revolution. Monseñor said to Milton Mendez:

---

72. "The Political Dimension of the Faith from the Perspective of the Option for the Poor," in Romero, *Voice of the Voiceless,* pp. 180–81 (emphasis added).
73. Ibid., p. 187.

Look, when the uprising happens, I don't want to be separate from or far away from the people. And I don't want to
be on the other side. . . . Of course, I would never take up
a weapon. I wouldn't be of any use in that arena. But I can
attend to the wounded and the dying, and I can gather up
the dead bodies. Right?[74]

At the invitation of Daniel Ortega and Miguel D'Escoto, the
Archbishop had purchased a ticket to visit revolutionary Nicaragua.
A priest named Astor Ruiz had gone to Nicaragua and then slipped
back into El Salvador. Romero urged him to return to Nicaragua
because, for the moment, "you won't be able to do anything here."
We need priests in reserve, Monseñor continued, so that when El
Salvador changes you can come back. "Your experience in Nicaragua
is going to be important for everybody. For me too. You know, we
really have to rethink the word I used to be so afraid of—the word
'revolution.' That word carries a lot of the Gospel in it." [75]

In an interview on March 19, 1980, with a Venezuelan newspaper
he said, "The so-called Left is the people. . . . We can't say that there is
a formula for moving from capitalism to socialism. If you want to call it
socialism, well, it's just a name. What we're looking for is justice, a kinder
society, a sharing of resources. That's what people are looking for."

The single best summary known to me of the practice of accompaniment as envisioned by Archbishop Oscar Romero is a portion
of the Campesino (Peasants') Mass apparently composed by pastoral
workers like Father Grande, together with their congregations, in
the mid and late 1970s. The last portion of the liturgy is the "*despedida*," or dismissal. In rough English translation, the *despedida* of the
Salvadoran Campesino Mass goes as follows:

When the poor come to believe in the poor
Then indeed we will be able to sing of liberty.
When the poor come to believe in the poor
We will construct fraternity.

Till we meet again, brothers!
The mass has ended

---

74. López Vigil, *Memories*, p. 351.
75. Ibid., pp. 393–94.

And we know what God told us.
Right now, yes, we are clear,
We are able to go forward,
We understand the task we must begin.

We are all committed
At the Lord's table
To construct a world of love,
To struggle with the brothers
To create community.
Christ lives in this solidarity.

When the poor seek out the poor
And organization is born
That's when our liberation begins.
When the poor make known to the poor
The hope that He gave us
That's when His kingdom
Is born among us.

The funeral mass for Archbishop Oscar Romero was interrupted by bomb explosions and sniper fire, prompting a pell-mell rush on the Cathedral. Most of the forty dead and two hundred wounded were older women.

In the midst of this chaos, Cardinal Corripio sought to finish the funeral liturgy.

"Give me the hosts so I can continue the Mass," Corripio said.

"There aren't any, your Excellency."

"Give me the wine."

"There isn't any."

"How about a prayer book, so we can at least do the responsorial prayers."

"There's no book either, your Excellency."

Then Samuel Ruiz, Bishop of Chiapas, took a little book of prayers out of his pocket, and they used that to say a few prayers before burying Monseñor.[76]

---

76. López Vigil, *Memories*, pp. 420–21.

Accompanying Prisoners

I. In Ohio (by Alice Lynd)

Getting Started

IN 1993, THERE WAS A MAJOR PRISON RIOT AT THE SOUTHERN OHIO Correctional Facility in Lucasville, Ohio.[1] Prisoners were seeking attention to their conditions of confinement. During the eleven-day uprising, nine prisoners and one correctional officer were killed. Nearly fifty prisoners were tried for riot-related offenses and five of them were sentenced to death. A large housing block was destroyed, and as a result many prisoners were transferred to other institutions.

Shortly thereafter, a former Legal Services client wrote to Staughton and me. He had been a prisoner in one of the prisons to which Lucasville prisoners were being transferred, and he was moved to a prison near us. He asked us to do the paperwork necessary to get on his visiting list. We did. We visited him once a month for six years until he was transferred to a prison too distant for us to visit. This is what started an increasingly complex and interrelated venture into what were for us previously unknown areas of the law and of human endurance.[2]

In response to the Lucasville riot, Ohio decided to build a supermaximum security prison, otherwise known as a "supermax," in Youngstown, approximately a half-hour drive from where we live. We were asked by people associated with the American Friends Service Committee to organize a protest to take place in March or April 1996.

My first step was to read every article I could find on supermax prisons and write a paper called "What Is a Supermax Prison?" I discovered that solitary confinement for an indefinite number of years is likely to cause mental health to deteriorate, in some instances resulting in violence to self or others.

---

1. See Staughton Lynd, *Lucasville: The Untold Story of a Prison Uprising* (Oakland, CA: PM Press, 2011).
2. See Lynd and Lynd, *Stepping Stones*, especially the chapter titled "The Worst of the Worst."

I shared my paper at a meeting of the Workers Solidarity Club to which we also invited members of the Youngstown Peace Council. About fifteen people came. We agreed that we should sponsor a community forum. Ohio's first private prison was being built by the Corrections Corporation of America at about the same time, so our forum focused on the private prison as well as the supermax. Both prisons had been sought by local officials to provide jobs after the closing of steel mills and loss of jobs in related industries such as trucking. About one hundred people came to our first "Prison Forum" at the little chapel within sight of the cranes where the Ohio State Penitentiary (OSP) was being built.

I wanted the program to include a speaker who had been held in solitary confinement for years or who was the relative of such a prisoner. We had both. The relative was the sister of George Skatzes (pronounced "skates"). George was a negotiator and spokesman for the prisoners during the Lucasville riot. He had been convicted of three murders and sentenced to death only a few weeks before the forum. His sister gave us the name of his lawyer and some of the documents related to his case. We began to visit George once a month also. Soon other men who were sentenced to death for alleged riot-related crimes began to send us their papers.

When the Ohio State Penitentiary opened in May 1998, among the first prisoners transferred to OSP were these men who already knew our address and who wrote to us about conditions there. George Skatzes was transferred during the second week. In June 1998, we visited him. It was the first visit to any prisoner in that institution. Although George was locked in a booth on one side of a solid glass panel and we were locked in the booth on the other side, George was shackled and his hands were cuffed behind his back. He sat on a stool for the entire duration of our visit, a couple of hours, with a correctional officer sitting just outside his side of the booth. The second time we visited George, his hands were locked at his waist with a device that held his right hand rigidly facing up and his left hand below it facing down, such that it was impossible to coordinate use of both hands, or so much as touch his own face.

At that time, prisoners had no property unless it was specifically authorized. They had only liquid soap in a plastic tube. "Never in my life have I been anywhere where I couldn't have a bar of soap!" George exclaimed. The Muslim prisoners complained that they were allowed only two paperback books and they needed three hardcover books for their religious observances. The prisoners could have no socks or T-shirts. And so it went: no . . . no . . . no.

There was no outdoor recreation. There was only an empty cell without recreation equipment in each "pod," which had holes on one side through which wind and rain could blow in. Later on, when Staughton took a deposition from the Director of the Ohio Department of Rehabilitation and Correction and asked why OSP was built with no outdoor recreation, he responded that the Lucasville riot began on the rec yard.

Prisoners were transferred to OSP without any notice or opportunity to file objections (contrary to administrative regulations), and before any policy was adopted to guide wardens as to who could be sent to the supermax prison. During the summer of 1998, I drafted an appeal form that many individual prisoners used.

One of the prisoners with whom I corresponded was of immense assistance to me in learning what the applicable rules and policies were. He explained to me the relevant provisions of the Rules Infraction Board policies. Whenever I drafted a form or a memo to prisoners, I would send it to him for comment before sending it to anyone else. He would write back and say, in effect, what you wrote is good but you should add.

Prisoners sent me copies of their grievances and the institutional inspector's or chief inspector's responses. I could see how the relevant policies were being applied and anticipate what to say to the next man who posed a similar problem. I learned from some prisoners what other prisoners needed to learn from me.

Suicides

By the summer of 1999, we were corresponding with approximately a hundred prisoners at OSP and were taking up various issues with the prison administration. Two prisoners had committed suicide. Before the second suicide, prisoners wrote to us expressing their concern about the way the guards were taunting this man after he returned from suicide watch and I had raised the issue with the administration. Then we got a phone call from the warden's assistant telling us the prisoner was dead. He asked us what we thought would give prisoners more desire to live. Staughton and I talked with him for an hour or so. After we hung up I said to Staughton, "He should be asking the prisoners, not us!"

So I drafted a form letter and sent it to the hundred prisoners who had written to us. I asked them, "What could OSP do to make you feel your life was more worth living?" I said, you don't have to answer if you don't want to, but if you do answer, write something that I can send in to the prison administration. You don't have to sign your name. I got 110 responses! I typed them up according to topic without identifying who said what. Some of the prisoners described their experiences of uncontrollable anger and desire to lash out. Some said it was like being in a tomb. Nearly all said, show us respect! Later, one wrote that what he needed was a copy of the book *Man's Search for Meaning.*

I sent the compilation of the men's responses not only to prison officials but also to various human rights organizations. One attorney responded. She and other attorneys who were familiar with conditions in supermax prisons in other states were of the opinion that you can't win much through litigation. However, our friend Jules Lobel, author of *Success Without Victory*, believed that even if you lose it is important to air major human rights issues in the courts and in public view.[3] One day, Jules asked us, "when are we going to do something about the supermax prison?"

Class Action

Jules asked me to prepare a legal memorandum demonstrating how we could overcome an initial hurdle. According to previous decisions of the United States Supreme Court, in order to be entitled to due process, prisoners had to prove that incarceration in the Ohio State Penitentiary was "an atypical and significant hardship as compared with the ordinary incidents of prison life."

Drawing on what had become a huge volume of letters, grievances, and perfunctory denials of security level reduction that prisoners had sent me over a period of nearly three years, I was able to produce the factual basis for the complaint that Jules and I drafted. When the case went to trial in January 2002, at one point the judge mused out loud, why would anyone rather be on death row than at OSP? We proved to the satisfaction of that District Court judge that conditions of confinement at OSP were an atypical and significant hardship. The Supreme Court of the United States later unanimously agreed.

---

3. See Jules Lobel, *Success Without Victory: Lost Legal Battles and the Long Road to Justice in America* (New York: New York University Press, 2003).

Elements of Accompaniment

What were we doing? We were listening. We were responding. We would look up regulations and tell the prison authorities when they were not following their own rules. We would tell the prisoners what procedures they could follow to lay the groundwork for challenging what was happening to them.

One prisoner would tell us about another who he thought was seriously mentally ill. We would go to see that man. After our lawsuit was filed, we scheduled one visit a week with a prisoner who we thought was seriously mentally ill. A few days later someone from mental health in Central Office would visit that same man and before long he was transferred to another prison. (I came to regard that as problem-shifting, not problem-solving!)

The judge allowed us to have two representatives of the prisoners in the courtroom during hearings. We met with them. We discussed issues and strategy with them. We sent them documents, and drafts of what we proposed to file. We provided expertise as lawyers and they provided expertise about what was happening to them.

We had a few meetings with as many as sixteen prisoners. The meetings took place in a pod where each man was locked in a separate cell with the food slot open so that he could hear and speak and, by putting his arm out through the slot, vote. At one such meeting, we presented to the prisoners a settlement proposed by the State's attorneys. Many of the prisoners did not know each other. One said he thought it would help him personally but it would not solve the problem, so he would vote against it. They decided unanimously to reject the settlement.

Within a few days, after the trial but before the judge had issued an opinion, another judge phoned us, urging us to go back to the prisoners and lean on them to accept the settlement. We said No. The prisoners had made their decision. They were aware that they were taking their chances but they would not agree to what had been offered. A few weeks later, the judge who had conducted the trial ruled in favor of the prisoners!

Another time, we had an issue that we thought was very important but we had reason to believe that the State would oppose any witness being heard on the subject. So we asked one of the regular prisoner representatives to let another man go to the hearing in his place. With the prospective witness present in the courtroom, the judge let him take the stand as a witness. The judge was outraged at what he heard! The State's attorneys soon took steps to change the policy.

We gave the prisoners the opportunity to speak for themselves, and they did. At times when the prisoners could not be present, we were their voice. Jason Robb, one of the prisoner representatives, recalls, "I remember the first time you both sang for me and a cell block full of convicts in a supermax prison! All these so-called hard core convicts and alleged menaces to society fell so silent as your voices rang out and all about this dark place, the officers all looking in amazement."

One Thing Leads to Another

Our work with prisoners began by visiting one prisoner, not about anything in particular, just visiting and listening to what he told us about tuberculosis in prisons, prison labor, anything and everything that he was observing.

Then we became aware of conditions of confinement in supermax prisons. That led to our getting to know George Skatzes. George made us aware of the "death qualified jury" that excludes people who oppose the death penalty from the jury in a capital case. He also told us about the use of unreliable "snitch testimony" to gain convictions and reward the witness by reduced or no charges, a letter to the Parole Board, or other benefits.

Because so many participants in the Lucasville riot were placed at the Ohio State Penitentiary near our home, it was easy for us to visit them. We got to know all of the prisoners sentenced to death for participating in the Lucasville riot, and then many who were not sentenced to death but were given very long sentences. We began to see that witnesses testified differently in different trials, and that often the facts on which juries and courts relied were contradictory or incomplete.[4]

In 2005, during the period of time when we represented every prisoner in the building, death row was transferred to the Ohio State Penitentiary. We got to know a lot of other men who were sentenced to death, which gave us a broader understanding of the flaws in the administration of the death penalty in Ohio.

---

4. See Staughton Lynd, "*Napue* Nightmares: Perjured Testimony in Trials Following the 1993 Lucasville, Ohio, Prison Uprising," *Capital University Law Review,* vol. 36, no. 3 (Spring 2008).

Furthermore, the men who were sentenced to death for murders that occurred during the Lucasville riot were still being held in solitary confinement on Ohio's highest security level, and denied privileges that men in the death row unit were allowed. Three of those men, two of whom had been representatives of the prisoners during the class action, went on hunger strike for approximately twelve days in January 2011. Although they were not transferred to the death row unit, their privileges were extended to match some of the death row privileges, such as semi-contact visits that make it possible to hold the hand of a loved one.

Throughout the time that the class action was in court, 2001–2008, prisoners in supermax prisons in other states contacted us. Among them were prisoners in the Security Housing Unit (SHU) at Pelican Bay in California. They sent us court cases on some of the same issues we were facing and I sent them documents illustrating what we had won.

Then, after the successful hunger strike at the Ohio State Penitentiary in 2011 that garnered international publicity and support, a considerable number of men at Pelican Bay presented their formal demands to the California prison authorities, seeking relief that in some cases had been ordered by courts but not provided, or that required changes in policy and procedures. When we showed the Pelican Bay demands to one of the OSP prisoners who had been both a representative during the class action and a hunger striker in 2011, he responded, "That's what we now have. We didn't used to but we do now."

We still hear from some prisoners who used to be at OSP but who have been reduced to lower security levels and transferred to other prisons. They raise issues related to overcrowding and insufficient medical care, issues similar to some of those at Lucasville before the riot.

We also hear from prisoners who say that we have opened their eyes to nonviolent ways of responding to the stressful situations in which they find themselves.

We attended a rally sponsored by Loved Ones of Prisoners at the beginning of the OSP hunger strike in January 2011. The leader of the group said she has a grandson on death row, "not like the Lynds who don't have any loved ones there." I responded, "Yes, we do. They just aren't relatives."

II. Ohio and California (by Staughton Lynd)

A common objection to the idea of accompaniment is that its successes are, at best, small-scale. We are asked: How can one expect
such tempests in scattered tea pots, such organizational small pota-
toes, to result in the deep structural changes in the broader society
that are required?

In fact, the recent history of the United States abounds in
small-scale actions that unexpectedly acted as "triggers" for multiple
imitation and widespread change. Some of the most critical moments
in the formation of industrial unions in the 1930s occurred when
small groups of men—tire builders in Akron, welders in the "body
in white" section of a General Motors plant in Flint—stopped work.
When Rosa Parks refused to go to the back of a bus in 1955, she could
not have foreseen what followed when a young black minister who
had just arrived in Montgomery, Martin Luther King, Jr., made his
church available for mass meetings. Four African-American college
students who "sat in" at a Greensboro, North Carolina, lunch counter
early in 1960 had no way of knowing that they would be imitated by
small groups all across the South, who then gathered together in April
to create the Student Nonviolent Coordinating Committee (SNCC).

Writing in 2011, it is self-evident that the triggering effect of
such exemplary small actions is not limited to the United States nor
in any way dependent on unique features of American culture or
social structure. A fruit seller who tragically burned himself to death
in Tunisia dislodged a landslide of social change across North Africa
and beyond.

Within the compass of our prison advocacy, we had occasion
to observe such a sequence of events involving first Ohio, and then
California.

When, in January 2011, three of the men sentenced to death after
the 1993 uprising in Lucasville, Ohio, carried out a successful hunger
strike at the Ohio State Penitentiary (OSP), the initiative of these
members of the "Lucasville Five" transcended racial boundaries.[5] This

---

5. George Skatzes had been transferred to the Mansfield Correctional
Institution (ManCI). James Were a.k.a. Namir Abdul Mateen had diabetes,
making it unwise for him to engage in a prolonged fast. Hence, although
all five men had taken part in hunger strikes together previously, only three
did so in 2011 at OSP.

was the product of a solidarity forged throughout almost twenty years of solitary confinement. Keith LaMar a.k.a. Bomani Shakur ("thankful mighty warrior" in Swahili) is an African American unaffiliated with any "gang." Jason Robb was a leader of the Aryan Brotherhood at Lucasville in 1993 and remains associated with the group. Keith and Jason were for years the joint representatives of the several hundred prisoners at Ohio's supermaximum security prison who brought the class action lawsuit, *Austin v. Wilkinson*. The third hunger striker was the Muslim imam, Siddique Abdullah Hasan, formerly known as Carlos Sanders. Thus the model that this activity offered to supermax prisons in California, often viewed as snakepits of racial and gang hostility, was a model of solidarity across racial and ethnic lines.

A second critical feature of the OSP hunger strike was that the hunger strikers won. Typically in a hunger strike, the physical resistance of the protesters wears down, some of the individuals involved are taken to hospital, prison representatives make illusory promises, and what began in solidarity dribbles away in individual withdrawal. As a result, hunger strikes in prison are almost always unsuccessful.[6] It is not entirely clear why the OSP action departed from this pattern of defeat, familiar to the Lucasville Five from previous frustrating hunger strikes. Some things are apparent. The demands of the OSP hunger strikers were modest. The three men sentenced to death for alleged activity at Lucasville in 1993 asked to be given the same privileges available to other men sentenced to death, confined in a different section of OSP. These privileges included the possibility of touching the hands of friends and relatives during "semi-contact" visits, and the opportunity to do computer research in the law.

The reverberation of a hunger strike victory among similarly situated prisoners elsewhere may be difficult for someone not confined behind bars to appreciate. Alice and I recall a conference in Washington, DC, that we attended early in our advocacy

---

6. However, conscientious objectors to World War II won important victories. David Dellinger tells how the warden at the Lewisburg maximum security penitentiary came to him during a hunger strike and said of David's wife Betty, "She's dying. She has sent a message telling you to go off the strike so that she can die in peace." After considerable internal turmoil, David concluded the warden was lying. He was. "Weeks later," the prisoners ended their strike after they won an end to censorship of their mail. David Dellinger, *From Yale to Jail: The Life Story of a Moral Dissenter* (New York: Pantheon Books, 1993), pp. 121–22.

for supermax prisoners. I remarked that lawyers for such prisoners should support the self-activity of the men themselves. This commonplace observation caused another lawyer to protest, "But these men are in supermax confinement: they can't *do* anything!" I silently commented to myself, "Oh yeah?" But self-activity in a supermax is extremely difficult. When Irish prisoners undertook hunger strikes in the 1980s, ten of them died.

Further, it is important to note that the decision of the Supreme Court in the Ohio case, while stopping far short of questioning the existence of supermax confinement, mandated certain procedural safeguards that were binding on such prisons throughout the United States. The justices stated unanimously that before a prisoner is placed in the "atypical and significant hardship" of supermax confinement, the inmate must receive notice in the form of "a brief summary of the factual basis" for that proposed placement and must be allowed "a rebuttal opportunity."[7] Moreover, when the case was remanded to the lower federal courts, the Ohio Department of Rehabilitation and Correction revised policy 53-CLS-04 so as to bring Ohio into compliance with *Wilkinson*'s directives. That policy, still in effect as these words are being written in August 2011, states that an inmate may not be placed at the highest level of security classification unless either a Rules Infraction Board or a court of law has found the prisoner guilty of committing one of a specified list of serious offenses.[8]

Supermax prisoners outside Ohio were anxious to learn the details of what had and had not been decided in *Wilkinson*. In California, a man could be locked down for decades on the uncorroborated say-so of other prisoners. For a prisoner in the Security Housing Unit (SHU) of the Pelican Bay supermax near the lonely border between California and Oregon, Justice Kennedy's words on behalf of a unanimous court in *Wilkinson* were like finding gold in a discouraging pile of loose pebbles.

Finally, Ohio was important because the Lynds had become friends with Denis O'Hearn, author of a moving and pathbreaking book about Bobby Sands and the other Irish hunger strikers.[9] Denis was adept in using the Internet and built a formidable international

---

7. *Wilkinson v. Austin*, 545 U.S. 209, 226 (2005).
8. Policy 53-CLS-04, effective Nov. 5, 2007, at VI(B) and (C).
9. O'Hearn, *Nothing but an Unfinished Song*.

network of support for the three Ohio hunger strikers. When Keith and Jason met with visitors during their hunger strike they would bring with them to the visiting booth packets of letters that had arrived from Great Britain, the Netherlands, Germany, Italy, Serbia, and points East. This was important because, like hunger strikers in Ohio, the Californians decided to forfeit the possibility of surprise and to create a public solidarity network for the action they were about to undertake *before* their hunger strike began on July 1, 2011.

The Pelican Bay prisoners began their dramatic concerted activity only after they had won significant victories in California federal courts but the state prison authorities had failed to change their policies. A federal judge found that Robert Lee Griffin had been held in solitary confinement in the Pelican Bay SHU for more than twenty years; that the sole justification for his segregation was his so-called "active" gang participation; that the State had presented no evidence of Mr. Griffin's active participation in a gang or knowledge of gang activity while confined in the SHU; and that the psychological harm sustained by Mr. Griffin's prolonged solitary confinement outweighed "the otherwise legitimate interest of prison officials in controlling prison gang activity." The judge ordered Mr. Griffin released from the SHU immediately.[10]

In a second case, the evidence used by the penal system to "validate" Ernesto Lira's membership in a gang included a drawing found in his possession depicting a "huelga bird."[11] "Huelga" is the Spanish word for "strike" and the symbolic bird is the logo of the United Farm Workers union.[12] Judge Illston found that none of the evidence used to validate Mr. Lira's solitary confinement was meaningful or reliable, and that his due process rights were violated when he was validated as a gang member without notice and an opportunity to present his views. But the penal system's administrators treated the Griffin and Lira cases merely as implicating individuals, and did nothing to change their general practices.

Accordingly, prisoners in the Pelican Bay SHU reported that inmates had been reading Thomas Paine, Howard Zinn, and Mayan cosmology, and "exploring the possibility of a rolling hunger strike." The strike would be based on "twenty-plus years of torture." The

---

10. *Griffin v. Gomez*, No. C98-21038 JW (N.D. Cal. June 28, 2006).
11. *Lira v. Cate*, No. C00-0095SI (N.D. Cal. Sept. 30, 2009).
12. Ibid., pp. 25–28.

feeling of the men was that they had nothing to lose by a peaceful protest even if taken "as far as necessary." More than fifty prisoners were said to have read Denis O'Hearn's book on the Irish hunger strikers of the 1980s, and it had a "big impact." And the Ohio victory, they wrote, "inspired us too—we feel the time is ripe!"

The idea of a strike was strongly supported by men in Pelican Bay's "short corridor" where the "worst of the worst of the worst" were housed. A large number were in their fifties and sixties. People with serious medical issues were not expected to participate.

By early April 2011, prisoners reported that twenty or thirty of them "aim to go all the way" and about fifty more had committed to go at least ten days. It was hoped that online postings and print periodicals would spread the word to prisoners elsewhere in California.

Meantime, prisoners had "collectively collaborated on five core demands." In summary, they were:

1. Group punishment must end. Each prisoner was to be evaluated on the basis of his individual rule violations.

2. The only way to get out of the SHU was to identify other prisoners as gang members or affiliates, a process known as "debriefing." The practice of "debriefing" was to be abolished. "Innocuous association" and allegations of gang activity by other prisoners were not to be considered.

3. Long-term solitary confinement should also be ended. Segregation should be a last resort. Inmates in the SHU must have adequate natural sunlight and quality health care.

4. There must be adequate food. Special diet meals were to be provided. Individuals must be allowed to purchase vitamin supplements. Food should not be used as a means of punishment.

5. Constructive programming was required for those on indefinite SHU status. Examples were: more visits, a weekly phone call, two annual packages, expanded canteen, more TV channels, hobby craft items, sweat suits and "watch caps," wall calendars, correspondence courses that require proctored exams. It was pointed out that such privileges are available to supermax prisoners in Florence, Colorado and Youngstown, Ohio, and denials based on safety and security are exaggerated.

Question was raised as to whether the core group of potential hunger strikers included members of all significant racial and ethnic groups. The answer was an unambiguous "Yes!" The makeup of the "short corridor" was 35 white, about 20 black, and 166 Hispanic. A group of about a dozen were selected to carry on negotiations, including, in approximately equal numbers, African Americans, Caucasians, Hispanics from Southern California, and Hispanics from Northern California.

Among the African Americans were two men who had been in the SHU more than twenty-five years and called themselves "New Afrikans." They had been denied release from the SHU because they possessed literature written by George Jackson and the Black Panthers, among others. Later, after the hunger strike had begun, a New Afrikan prisoner was transferred out of Pelican Bay on the eve of a negotiating session with the authorities. A representative of Northern California Hispanics reported:

> We insisted that we would not go out to meet with them unless there was a New Afrikan representative. The [correctional officer] made several trips explaining our position. Then the associate warden K.L. McGuyer came down himself along with Captain Wood. They asked one of the negotiators would they agree to meet with undersecretary Scott Kernan, tomorrow. . . . The negotiators said only if a substitute New Afrikan could take the place of the one you all transferred abruptly. He said yes!

By early June, there was hope that the hunger strike might include at least two hundred prisoners in other Security Housing and administrative segregation units in California, and would become "the largest hunger strike protest in U.S. history." The five demands, together with a cover letter and a formal complaint filed in compliance with the prison grievance system, were sent to Governor Jerry Brown, the secretary of the California Department of Corrections and Rehabilitation, and the warden.

About a week into the hunger strike, a letter said that "we've gotten a ton of fantastic support from . . . thousands of people around the world." As he was writing, the author continued,

> [t]here's a support rally going on in front of the court house in Eureka, which is approximately 90 miles south of here!!

On Friday and Saturday there was a small group of supporters out in front of this place. They came from the L.A. area
and were dressed in full Mayan dress, beating a drum and
chanting support slogans. Guys could hear it when out in
the little dog-run yards!

Prison authorities were trying to downplay what was going on,
we were told. They were saying that "there were only 12 to 25 guys
refusing to eat a meal," when in reality *more than six thousand* men in
many different prisons had gone on hunger strike "for at least a day
to show support." In the short corridor at Pelican Bay there were still
about 120 (of the original 145) men going without food. Several men
had been taken to hospital. Others were warned in graphic detail by
the examining medical personnel about what could happen to a human being who went without food.

A letter from Bomani (Keith LaMar) at OSP had been received
and "everyone was impressed and welcomed" it. A visiting attorney
had been asked "to be sure that they show support for the OSP men
fighting the death penalty sentences!! The OSP hunger strike was
part of what motivated us!!"

"We're hoping for some response from CDCR [California
Department of Corrections and Rehabilitation] headquarters this
week," a correspondent concluded. "But [we] expect it may still come
to some deaths before they act right."

"Accompaniment"

"Accompaniment" is actually an umbrella term that includes a family
of related practices: equality, listening, seeking consensus, and exemplary action. The formation of a support coalition outside the walls,
like self-organization within the Pelican Bay SHU, illustrates the
convergence of these practices.

The equality of all participants is foundational. If an organizer
considers that he or she already knows not only the objective to
be sought but how to get there, there is no reason to give equal
importance to the people being organized. Listening, under these
circumstances, will be merely tactical, asking the question: Is there
enough support "out there" for our preplanned campaign to succeed?

An altogether different atmosphere comes into being if there
is mutual recognition that no one has all the answers and that it

is accordingly necessary to search together so that (in the Quaker phrase) "way may open." Listening then becomes intense and may be prolonged. The desired place of arrival will be consensus. However, should consensus not emerge, instead of maneuvering to win a vote the next step is likely to be a time in which individuals or small groups act out perceived images of the road ahead. The process will be understood in the manner of the Biblical parable of sowing. We ourselves are the seed that is thrown onto various kinds of soil. Whether or not something grows and flourishes is not so much a test of our abilities as an experiment, the results of which, whether good or ill, will contribute to the common store of understanding.

These processes were at work as support built for the impending July 1 start date of the hunger strike. For potential outside supporters just as for prisoners in the SHU, awareness of the Ohio victory boosted morale. A Pelican Bay activist told a staff attorney for California Prison Focus, "Outside supporters are critical. In the Ohio SuperMax hunger strike, 1,200 supporters' names were given to the governor and prison authorities. The strikers got all their demands met after *twelve days*."

A meeting of potential supporters on June 1 adopted the name "Prisoner Hunger Strike Solidarity." The following ground rules for decision making were adopted:

a. Striving to arrive at decisions through consensus.
b. Absent a consensus, majority rules.
c. Organizations absent from the meeting must be informed before taking important votes.
d. No single group will/should put their own name forward or organization ahead of the group.
e. Everyone is assumed to be working for the common good. If someone makes a mistake, stress forgiveness.
f. Decisions or opinions that are requested of the group assume a twenty-four-hour response time.
g. Smaller workgroups or committees are empowered to make decisions to carry out tasks, but important/key decisions must be brought to the group for a decision.

Particular substantive decisions made at the same meeting showed concern to follow the lead of the prisoners themselves and to reach out to prisoners' families. The new organization described itself as "a coalition of grass roots activist organizations seeking to give voice to prisoners in Pelican Bay SHU going on hunger strike." Information sheets about the hunger strike were to be sent to "four family of prisoners blogs." Under the subhead "Prisoners asked us to propose a mediator," the meeting minutes reported discussion as to whether the mediator should be a single person or a team. A five-person team resulted.

These Sixties-style proceedings expanded during the month before July 1. Haribu L.M. Soriano-Mugabi, a prisoner in the supermax section of Corcoran state prison, reported that he and his colleagues were in full support of the July 1 action "and the 5 major action points." The *Prison Focus* newsletter, no. 37 (summer 2011), printed the Formal Complaint of "SHU Short Corridor Inmates" signed by seven representatives, and a number of letters. A press conference in Oakland was announced for June 30.

July 1 brought forth a flood of publicity. On July 5, the coalition asserted that "at least 6 state prisons have joined in." The *New York Times* reported that, according to the California Department of Corrections and Rehabilitation, 6,600 prisoners took part in the hunger strike during the July 4 weekend and on July 7 "about 1,700 prisoners . . . were continuing to refuse at least some state-issued meals." Also on July 7, according to the *Los Angeles Times*, "Inmates in at least 11 of California's 33 prisons are refusing meals in solidarity."

The biggest publicity breakthrough began with an Op-Ed in the *New York Times* entitled "Barbarous Confinement." Three supportive letters followed a week later. Then on August 2, under the heading "Cruel Isolation," the lead editorial in the *Times* noted that nationwide "more than 20,000 inmates are confined in 'supermax' facilities under horrid conditions." The editorial concluded that "decency requires limits. Resorting to a dehumanizing form of punishment well known to induce suffering and drive people into mental illness is beyond them."

An important addition to the critique appearing in the *New York Times* was a story in the *Sacramento Bee* on August 18. The newspaper reported as fact that the state "had tried to tamp down the protest by moving 17 hunger strike leaders to the state prison in Corcoran." The result, according to corrections spokesman Oscar Hidalgo, was that "an additional 300 prisoners at that institution went on the hunger strike."

Amid this barrage of supportive publicity, prisoners accepted a truce, or what one of them termed a "brief grace period," to give the authorities time to begin to reverse the present policy of "validation" and "debriefing." The prisoner representatives made it clear that they were prepared to resume the hunger strike if necessary. Prisoners involved in the negotiations wrote to the support coalition reminding them that they wished to be called "representatives," not leaders. A major issue in California, as in Ohio, is that members of the media are not permitted to speak with insurgent inmates.

The last scene in Act One of this drama was a crowded legislative hearing in Sacramento on August 23. The day began with lobbying. At 11:30, there was a rally. The hearing began at 1:30 p.m. Former prisoners, relatives of prisoners, experts on the psychological effects of prolonged isolation, an attorney for prisoners in the SHU, a representative of teachers in support of better education programs in the SHU, a minister and a spokesperson for the American Friends Service Committee, all had an opportunity to testify to legislators many of whom seemed sympathetic. It was established that 435 people have served indeterminate sentences in the SHU for more than a decade, and 78 have been there for more than twenty years.

The Corrections Secretary of the California department testified as well. He said that a recent decision of the U.S. Supreme Court on overcrowding in California prisons made it possible for the authorities to begin to implement what had been recommended by a panel of experts in 2007. Those recommendations centered on moving to a conduct-based model that punishes inmates for tangible offenses, rather than for mere affiliation with a gang. The comparable regulations of twenty-eight states in which there are supermax prisons are being reviewed.

Prisoners at the Pelican Bay SHU and comparably restrictive areas of other California prisons renewed their hunger strike on September 26, 2011. The number of protesting inmates initially involved was even larger than in July, apparently numbering more than twelve thousand. This time hunger striking prisoners on the short corridor were removed to bare cells in the Administrative Segregation block. Not only were customary privileges, like TV, unavailable. Cold air was pumped through the cells continuously so that, even with two or three blankets and wearing every article of clothing provided, prisoners were always cold and had great difficulty sleeping. Visits with lawyers were delayed and then interrupted after only a few minutes of precious conversation. Physical symptoms accumulated together with a steady loss of weight.

Negotiations ending the renewed hunger strike were initiated by a memorandum from the prisoner representatives to Scott Kernan, the principal negotiator for the State. This led to a conference between Mr. Kernan and members of a "mediation team" who were trusted by the prisoners. On October 13, 2011, a written agreement was signed by the mediators after consultation with prisoner representatives, and by Mr. Kernan. The agreement reaffirmed the previously promised reconsideration of validation and debriefing policies, promised that the file of each prisoner in the SHU would be reviewed under the new criteria, that "those who are not re-validated under the new criteria will be released to general population," and that "those who are re-validated [under] the new criteria will still be able to advance out of the SHU via a stepdown program based on behavior." Mr. Kernan showed (but did not give) the members of the mediation team a thirty to thirty-five-page draft of proposed changes that was under consideration. The mediation team members affirmed that they had consulted Pelican Bay Hunger Strike representatives and could verify "that they decided to end the hunger strike."

Conclusion

The California hunger strike of 2011 was a spectacularly large mass movement initiated and controlled wholly from below. During the first phase of the strike, the California authorities negotiated directly with an interracial group of prisoner representatives. The movement received well-coordinated outside support and dramatic favorable publicity. It should be viewed as an exemplary demonstration of accompaniment.

Participants struggled with the ongoing difference between two timetables: on the one hand, the ability of middle-aged prisoners to go without food beyond a period of about three weeks; on the other hand, the inertia of a massive government bureaucracy, and its difficulty, like that of a battleship in midocean, in dramatically changing course.[13]

---

13. A hunger striker states: "The oldest man in the Ad/Seg icebox cells was 66, Danny [Troxell] was next at 58, the youngest two were 38. " However, this prisoner adds: "The 66 year old didn't look phased by day 18, and he reminded us before we went to the phone conference [with the mediators] what was at stake!!"

But one thing seems reasonably clear. We closed our consideration of accompaniment in El Salvador with the words that begin the dismissal to the campesino mass, "When the poor come to believe in the poor." Somewhat in the same vein, the letters of prisoners who experienced the Pelican Bay hunger strike appear to articulate the idea: whether the authorities have changed is open to question, nevertheless we have changed.

A representative of the prisoners reported that, as the second hunger strike approached an end, he was very much affected by a visit, interrupted by the authorities after five minutes, with a lawyer sympathetic to the protesting inmates "who was so concerned and compassionate and told me more than 12,000 people went on hunger strike in support." This was "very overwhelming and I was physically hurting that day and not used to folks truly caring!!" Then, when the same man was taken back to the AdSeg tier to which he and others had been moved, "all fourteen men were at their windows with looks of hope for some good news. It was directly akin to [Denis O'Hearn's] description of how the men acted in the H Block when Bobby Sands returned from some of his meetings."

A thoughtful letter from another prisoner during the hunger strike expressed a number of criticisms. Seven cells in his pod were still "going strong." But the strike didn't seem as strong and united as in July. "Many believe that the first strike was the time to push, go all the way till the main demands were met." Disciplinary action seemed likely at the end of the second strike but "it's just 90 days loss of privileges (TV or canteen)." The writer was "feeling more tired as the strike continues, but mentally I feel all right and my spirits solid last I checked."

The prisoner continued, "I was thinking earlier in the day how people in prison and outside postpone living."

> There's a higher purpose in life for all humans. We just have to find our place in the world being a positive force, and promote change and compassion naturally. How easy it is to deal with adversity and suffering when we are open and generous with ourselves and others.

A third prisoner wrote, "Please let it be known out there how deeply appreciative [we are about] the overwhelming way in which everyone very publicly rejected CDCR's propaganda of 'the worst of the worst' and demanded that we were/are much more than the crimes we've been convicted of or prison gang labels." Continuing, this man may have spoken for all his colleagues when he said, "I think that's even fundamentally changed the way many of us in here see ourselves now. We've all collectively shattered 30–35 years of CDCR status quo in three months. We should be proud of that."

Occupying the Future

Accompanying and Occupying

"Accompanying" and "occupying" are first cousins, or perhaps, to speak more precisely, blood brothers.

That is, when people set out to walk together as equals, to "make the road by walking," there is likely to grow from that horizontal companionship a shared desire for more enduring arrangements. The thoughts of the fellow travelers will turn toward establishing beachheads or bases of operations.

Thus in Brazil, it seems, students who set out to teach the children of agricultural laborers found themselves colleagues in efforts literally to occupy unused farmland. In Chiapas, a quasi-military operation launched from remote mountain enclaves turned into the persistent creation, in plain view, of a network of Zapatista villages.

Because of this predictable sequence of events, one can also think of stages in a process. First, we occupy and get to know each other. Then we pause and take ongoing control of some patch of reality so as to make possible further joint activity. Every form of protest discussed in previous chapters can be gathered into this paradigm. Thus, for example, one Occupier writes, "A thoughtful soldier, a soldier with a conscience, is the 1%'s worst nightmare."[1]

With regard to Occupy Wall Street specifically, something is known about how it came into being. There will be those who say that OWS was, in fact, "organized." But it seems to me more accurate to speak, not of organizers, but of initiators: people who set in motion a chain of events they would have been the first to describe as essentially unpredictable.

What may be characterized as the prehistory of Occupy Wall Street began in February 2010, when David DeGraw released a six-part online report and call to action entitled "The Economic Elite vs. The People of the United States of America."[2] The segments had titles like "Time for a Second American Revolution—The 99% Movement."

---

1. "The War Comes Home," *The Occupied Wall Street Journal* (November 2011), p. 2.
2. The following account of the prehistory of Occupy Wall Street follows David DeGraw, "Economic Elite Vs. The People: 99% Movement Call to Action Two Year Anniversary," February 15, 2012, http://ampedstatus.org/economic-elite-vs-the-people-99-movement-call-to-action-two-year-anniversary-book-release/.

DeGraw was anxious to revive the spirit of the early 1960s. The introduction to the series ended with the famous lines of Mario Savio:

> There's a time when the operation of the machine becomes so odious—makes you so sick at heart—that you can't take part. . . . And you've got to put your bodies upon the gears and upon the wheels, upon the levers, upon all the apparatus, and you've got to make it stop.

After a year of furious Internet exchanges, DeGraw explicitly called for what he termed "The Empire State Rebellion." He himself had lived for some time just around the corner from Zuccotti Park in lower Manhattan. It seemed to him fitting and proper to ask "millions of people to flood into lower Manhattan and camp out" there. By this time many Internet voices had joined in. The date on which the "decentralized nonviolent resistance movement" would appear on Wall Street was to be Flag Day, June 14, 2011.

DeGraw considered that with "hundreds of thousands of people engaged online" it was realistic to hope for a turnout of three hundred people. In fact only about sixteen showed up. Dismayed by the fact that media representatives outnumbered protesters, most of the sixteen left, leaving only four.

It was crunch time. There was no organization in being to decide, What next? Looking back, DeGraw comments, "The fact is we are all leaders. Unless everyone looks into the mirror and finds the leader within," the movement will fail. What actually happened was that another Internet network, called Adbusters, picked up the baton and called for a rerun, same idea, same place, three months later.

Adbusters magazine in Vancouver, British Columbia, put up a poster and a listserv in July 2011 that was "sent out to our 90,000-strong culture-jammers network around the world. It was also a blog post on our website." *Adbusters* cofounder and editor-in-chief Kalle Lasn explained:

> After Tunisia and Egypt, we were mightily inspired by the fact that a few smart people using Facebook and Twitter can put out calls and suddenly get huge numbers of people to get out into the streets and start giving vent to their anger. And then we keep on looking at the sorry state of the

political left in the United States and how the Tea Party is passionately strutting their stuff while the left is sort of hiding somewhere. We felt that there was a real potential for a Tahrir moment in America (a) because the political left needs it and (b) because people are losing their jobs, people are losing their homes, and young people cannot find a job. We felt that the people who gave us this mess—the financial fraudsters on Wall Street—haven't even been brought to justice yet. We felt that this was the right moment to instigate something.[3]

Mr. Lasn went on to explain that *Adbusters* editors are "students of the Situationist movement." The Situationists, he continued, were "the people who gave birth to what many think was the first global revolution back in 1968 when some uprisings in Paris suddenly inspired uprisings all over the world." The concept was that if you have a very powerful idea and the moment is ripe, "that is enough to start a revolution."

The *Adbusters* spokesperson added that he and other original instigators "thought that the idea of one demand was very important." Then there emerged the vision of a "leaderless, demandless movement." In Lasn's eyes it was a wonderful debate, each side making some good points. In his opinion the movement was "fine the way it is." Specific demands would emerge after "debates have been had in cities all around the world."

There remains the possibility that as so often in the past the "whole movement may fizzle out in a bunch of loony lefty kind of bullshit." But there is also a "deeper level of debate" that causes Kalle Lasn to be very hopeful. He describes it as "a different kind of mentality that young people have, a horizontal way of thinking about things, . . . a new model of democracy, a new model of how activism can work . . . that in some strange way works like the Internet works."

According to the *Adbusters* editor, a movement that focuses on one or a few powerful demands from below and a movement that demonstrates a new model of democracy are not "mutually exclusive."

---

3. Justin Elliott, "The Origins of Occupy Wall Street Explained: Salon Talks to the Editor of *Adbusters* about the Practical and Philosophical Roots of the Movement," Oct. 4, 2011, http://politics.salon.com/2011/10/04/adbusters_occupy_wall_st/singleton/.

The next steps in the process that led to Zuccotti Park in New York City have been described by anarchist anthropologist David Graeber. He says that on August 2, 2011, he "showed up at a 7 PM meeting at Bowling Green" that "a Greek anarchist friend, who I'd met at a recent anarchist get together . . . , told me was meant to plan some kind of action on Wall Street in mid-September." The meeting had been called by "a coalition top-heavy with NGOs, unions and socialist groups" that was trying "to take possession of" the idea floated by *Adbusters*.[4]

But as he paced about the Green, Graeber continued, he spotted several individuals that he knew from previous protest events and street battles.

> [T]his wasn't really a crowd of verticals—that is, the sort of people whose idea of political action is to march around with signs under the control of one or another top-down protest movement. They were mostly pretty obviously horizontals: people more sympathetic with anarchist principles of organization, non-hierarchical forms of direct democracy, and direct action.

Graeber and his friends decided not to surrender the evening to the "verticals."

> So we . . . formed a circle, and tried to get everyone else to join us. . . . We created a decision-making process (we would operate by modified consensus), broke out into working groups (outreach, action, facilitation) and then reassembled to allow each group to report its collective decisions, and set up times for new meetings of both the smaller and the larger groups.

There were obvious problems. There were only six weeks before the projected start date, "not nearly enough time to plan a major action, let alone bus in the thousands of people that would be required

---

4. David Graeber, "On Playing by the Rules—The Strange Success of Occupy Wall Street," October 19, 2011, http://www.nakedcapitalism.com/2011/10/david-graeber-on-playing-by-the-rules-%E2%80%93-the-strange-success-of-occupy-wall-street.html.

to actually shut down Wall Street." Besides, Wall Street could not be shut down on the date announced by *Adbusters*, September 17, because that was a Saturday. And the group had "no money of any kind."

Two days later, the Outreach committee met for brainstorming. Someone picked up the rhetoric of DeGraw's Call to Action and suggested: why not call ourselves the 99 percent? The formulation had been endorsed by, among others, Joseph Stiglitz, a Nobel Prize winner and formerly lead economist for the World Bank. The 1 percent are the super rich. The 99 percent are everybody else. Stiglitz had written in May 2011 that one percent of the U.S. population receives nearly a quarter of the national income and controls 40 percent of the country's wealth.[5]

An "emerging group" began to meet regularly at Tompkins Park. It was determined to create a New York General Assembly, on the model of previous gatherings in Europe. There was awareness that, thanks to the forty thousand members of the city police, Wall Street was probably the "single most heavily policed public space" in the world. The greatest concern during those "hectic weeks" was how to avoid a "total fiasco, with all the enthusiastic young people immediately beaten, arrested, and psychologically traumatized." There were ongoing struggles with hardcore anarchists on the Left who denounced the proposed action as reformist, and verticals on the Right who wanted to create a formal leadership structure.

Reflecting in wonder on the success beyond all dreams of what he helped to instigate, Graeber asks: so what did we do right this time? He identifies the core constituency of the occupations as college graduates, often of working-class background, who played by the rules and now find themselves burdened with college debt and unable to find work. He gives highest praise to these dogged young activists who dug themselves in and refused to leave.

He points to something else as well.[6] At the very first meeting on August 2, he relates, the "anarchists in the circle made what seemed, at the time, an insanely ambitious proposal: Why not let them operate exactly like this committee: by consensus?" As far as any of them

---

5. Joseph E. Stiglitz, "Of the 1% by the 1% for the 1%," *Vanity Fair* (May 2011).
6. David Graeber, "Enacting the Impossible: On Consensus Decision Making," October 23, 2011, http://occupiedmedia.us/2011/10/enacting-the-impossible/.

knew, he went on, nothing like this had ever been tried in a mass assembly like that anticipated in New York. But "we took the leap," and it worked in hundreds of assemblies across the country. And so he now asks, "how many other 'impossible' things might we pull off?"

The foregoing was the main stream of activity that led hundreds of participants to appear at a park in downtown Manhattan in September 2011. But the ongoing Occupations contain a variety of rivulets, arising in many different places rather than from a single spring.

Again, consider veterans. A preceding chapter in this book argued that volunteer soldiers could become conscientious objectors to further involvement in a particular war they were fighting. It appears that Scott Olsen, seriously injured at Occupation Oakland on October 25, 2011, was just such a soldier. Born in Wisconsin, Olson had volunteered for the Marines and served two tours in Iraq. While there he started a website called "I hate the Marine Corps" and received an "administrative discharge." After Olson was beaten at the site of Occupation Oakland, fracturing his skull and causing possible brain damage, veterans formed a group calling itself "Veterans of the 99 Percent" and individual veterans began to appear in large numbers at other Occupy gatherings.[7]

Similarly, of course, a plethora of trade unionists have responded to this student and ex-student initiative and joined Occupy events all over the United States.

At Occupy Youngstown

At the first gathering of Occupy Youngstown, on October 15, 2011, I made a few remarks about three things: 1. Solidarity; 2. Demands; 3. Life among the 99 Percent.

SOLIDARITY. We feel solidarity with Occupy Wall Street, and rejoice that they maintain their physical presence at their chosen park.

We feel solidarity with the many, many Occupy This Town and Occupy That Town that have sprung up, spontaneously, all over the United States: all over this land that suddenly seems more like "your land" and "my land," like our land, again.

---

7. Amy Goodman, "Call of Duty: Veterans Join the 99%," Truthdig, November 1, 2011; "Vets Swell Occupy Ranks after Injury," *USA Today*, November 2, 2011, p. 3A.

We feel solidarity with the occupation protests taking place to-day all over the world.

There is also solidarity over time. As a representative of Survivors Of the Sixties—acronym, SOS—I feel this kind of solidarity strongly.

Many of you have heard of Abbie Hoffman. He was in Mississippi, in 1967 he promoted the levitation of the Pentagon, and together with Jerry Rubin he started the Yippies.

I met Abbie twice. The first time was during the Chicago Democratic Party Convention, when I saw him wearing a black T-shirt, lying face down on a cot, in a Chicago city jail. The second time, more than twenty years later, was in a Franciscan church in Managua, Nicaragua. There is a part of the Catholic liturgy known as the "Peace of Christ" when each congregant greets others. At the church of St. Mary of the Angels one circled the floor, greeting elderly women, small of stature, many holding photographs of their sons who had been killed in the contra war.

Suddenly a bearded figure bounded across the floor from the other side of the church and embraced me. It was Abbie.

Not long afterward, he committed suicide. Tom Hayden commented, "We are all waiting for the new Movement. I guess Abbie couldn't wait any longer."

Try to imagine what the past three weeks, this moment of awakening, this vista of new hope, would have meant to the trail-blazers of the 1960s, to Dave Dellinger and Howard Zinn, to Stokely Carmichael and Jim Forman, to Barbara Deming.

Think also of Youngstown, Ohio, in the 1970s and 1980s, and the men and women who fought to substitute worker-community ownership for capitalist greed in what is today (October 2011) the poorest city in the nation. Think of Bishop James Malone, of Ed Mann who led us down the hill to occupy the U.S. Steel administration building, and his comrade, John Barbero. Think of Delores Hrycyk, wife of an LTV Steel retiree. Long before Facebook and Twitter, when LTV declared bankruptcy Delores called all the local radio stations and said there would be a retiree rally, here in Federal Plaza, just as today at noon on Saturday. A thousand people came. A retiree direct action movement, Solidarity USA, was born.

Think of Bob Vasquez, president of Steelworkers local union 1330 at U.S. Steel. Bob said, "We lost, but my members told me over and over again that we fought, and because we fought, we preserved our dignity."

Finally, in the 1990s there came, first, the Zapatista insurrection in Chiapas, and then, from 1999 to 2001, what Naomi Klein has described as "the last time a global, youth-led, decentralized movement took direct aim at corporate power." Back then, I felt that our protest activity was "summit-hopping." Two young men stayed overnight in our basement who had been in Seattle, went back to Chicago but were unsure what to do next, and were on their way to Quebec. Speaking to the general assembly at Occupy Wall Street, Naomi Klein described how the new movement is different.

> Occupy Wall Street, on the other hand, has chosen a fixed target. And you have put no end date on your presence here. This is wise. Only when you stay put can you grow roots. This is crucial. It is a fact of the information age that too many movements spring up like beautiful flowers but quickly die off. It's because they don't have roots. And they don't have long term plans for how they are going to sustain themselves. So when storms come, they get washed away.
>
> Being horizontal and deeply democratic is wonderful. But these principles are compatible with the hard work of building structures and institutions that are sturdy enough to weather the storms ahead. I have great faith that this will happen.[8]

DEMANDS. The pundits, the commentators, the talking heads, have one fundamental criticism of Occupy Wall Street: What are its demands? How can you have a movement without a specific program of things you are demanding?

They know not what they ask! Speaking for myself, I don't demand a list of specifics, I demand a qualitatively different kind of society. I seek the Kingdom of God on earth. I want to go back to the Book of Leviticus, chapter 25, declare a Year of Jubilee and wipe out all debts. But since I am a practical, moderate sort of fellow, I say: Let's begin by declaring an end to student indebtedness, so that young people can pursue their dreams rather than go to work for corporate law firms in order to pay down their loans.

I think Jubilee *is* a practical program. Twenty years ago, my wife Alice and I were in some of the few Syrian villages that remain in

---

8. Naomi Klein, "Occupy Wall Street: The Most Important Thing in the World Now," *The Nation*, October 6, 2011.

the Golan Heights, occupied in 1967 by the State of Israel. People there make a living by growing apples. And the villagers told us, "We don't understand this idea of fixed property boundaries. Families vary in size from one generation to the next, and therefore, we adjust the amount of land allotted to a particular family, depending on the number of mouths to be fed."

At present, although few of us live in gated communities, this whole society lives with gated imaginations. Each of us is encouraged to build a little island of personal financial security surrounded by an electrified fence. The fence keeps others out and keeps each of us imprisoned.

But OK, we might agree to postpone the Kingdom of God for a little while longer. It's already been delayed two thousand years. And there are a couple of things that need to be done right now, in Ohio, that we should demand.

One is to abolish the death penalty. Friends, the ice is breaking. Not long ago, Ohio executed more men every year than any other state except Texas. In 2010, Ohio was the only state in the nation that deliberately killed more human beings than it had murdered the year before. Presently, with to be sure a pause for Christmas, executions in Ohio are scheduled every month or two into the year 2013.

But the ice *is* breaking. Paul Pfeifer, the senior judge on the Ohio Supreme Court who helped to draft Ohio's capital punishment statute, has come out for abolishing the death penalty. Terry Collins, who as head of the Ohio Department of Rehabilitation and Correction witnessed more than thirty executions, has come out for abolishing the death penalty. Former Ohio Attorney General Jim Petro and his wife have written a book about miscarriages of justice in Ohio courts. There has been introduced in the Ohio House of Representatives a bill, H.B. 160, to abolish the death penalty and substitute life imprisonment without parole. I can only say: Come, Lord, quickly come.

These are objectives of highest priority.

But I want to make a final observation about demands. When our critics use the word "demands," they mean: tell some legislator or administrator what you want him or her to do for you. Gather your own initiative, your self-activity, and your righteous outrage into a bundle, and give it to someone else to act in your place. Tell somebody else what you want them to do for you.

But I say: Yes, we should vote. Yes, we should support this bill and oppose that one. Yes, we should give President Obama some pressure from what Subcomandante Marcos calls "below and to the Left," and thereby give the president some excuse to do what, in his heart of hearts, he no doubt often would really like to do.

But this is not our highest priority. Our most urgent objective is not to give someone else the authority to act on our behalf. Our greatest need is not to hand over to somebody other than ourselves the responsibility to remake the world.

No, we need to remake the world ourselves, right now, from below and to the Left. I am appalled at the poverty of imagination that has been shown in the last thirty years in the Mahoning Valley regarding what is to be done. A "shrinking city"? What kind of development strategy is that for a community that is already losing its young people? Tearing down buildings without knowing what to put in their place? Give me a break. A bulldozer can do that. It is not a plan of action, a vision, worthy of human beings.

The Chamber of Commerce is anxious to obliterate the memory of Youngstown's militant labor history. There used to be a plaque, right here in Federal Plaza, commemorating the Little Steel Strike of 1937. When the streets through downtown were reconfigured for the fifth or sixth time, the plaque disappeared. Don't worry, Staughton, I am told, it's in a museum. Yeah, I answer, and that's precisely the problem.

The fact is that new ideas are up and about in the Mahoning Valley but not in corporate boardrooms or in the corridors of power. One example of a program that needs to be supported and developed is the idea of providing much of the Valley's food with produce grown locally. Let me be blunt: this is a wonderful idea. But it must become an activity that offers full-time employment to young people trying to grow up and survive in the inner city, or it will remain a middle-class fad, and those young people will leave the area in desperation or wind up behind bars.

LIFE AMONG THE 99 PERCENT. In the late 1960s it was the thing to do to call police officers "pigs." I objected at the time, and I strongly object now. When I visit the state's first supermaximum security prison on Youngstown-Hubbard Road, often a correctional officer will call out, "Hello, Staughton! Remember me? I used to be your client." Steelworkers and truck drivers who have been unable to find work wind up in the Valley's many new prisons.

If we wish truly to be the 99 percent, we cannot call each other names. Barbara Deming had a good way of putting it. She said:

nature gives us two hands. With one of them, we must hold up a barrier to those we perceive as oppressors, and say: no further, or only over my body. With the other hand we must reach out to those same people and say: join us.[9]

The Lynds have on their kitchen wall some words attributed to KOR, a support group for Polish Solidarity.

> Start doing the things you think should be done.
> Start being what you think society should become.
> Do you believe in freedom of speech? Then speak freely.
> Do you love the truth? Then tell it.
> Do you believe in an open society? Then act in the open.
> Do you believe in a decent and humane society? Then behave decently and humanely.[10]

---

9. Barbara Deming, "On Revolution and Equilibrium," in *Nonviolence in America: A Documentary History*, revised edition (Maryknoll, NY: Orbis Books, 1995), ed. Staughton and Alice Lynd, p. 416.

10. KOR stands for Workers' Defense Committee. Members of KOR provided financial, legal, and medical assistance to workers and their families who were suffering from government repression. This summary of KOR's guiding principles appeared in "Reflections[,] A Better Today" by Jonathan Schell, *New Yorker* (February 3, 1986), p. 60.

Conclusion

THE PRACTICE OF ACCOMPANYING WILL NOT, IN ITSELF, TAKE US from where we are to that "otro mundo," or "other world," that the Zapatistas have encouraged us to imagine.

It is painful for me not to present a formula for getting from here to there, for creating an American socialism, for building another world. All I am sure about is a first step.

That first step, which I have called "accompanying," will require many of us on the Left to abandon preoccupation with a novel vocabulary, or a new organization. Instead this book proposes that it should become an expected first step for radical professionals and intellectuals, instead of spending their adulthood in enclaves on the East Coast, West Coast, or Great Lakes, to venture forth into relationships of companionship with ordinary people in places where there may be very few fellow radicals.

If my wife and I have added anything to this general notion it is that such an undertaking will go better if those setting out to "accompany" bring with them a skill that ordinary people need. Alice and I are products of the East Coast upper middle class (although a generation back, three of our four parents were born or grew up in the Midwest). My father and mother were tenured professors. There is no way in the world I could have come to be regarded as a useful resident of Youngstown, Ohio, had I not brought with me the credentials of a lawyer and a particular interest in employment law. Alice established a similar valued place, first as a paralegal working with disabled clients, then, after going to law school, among steel industry retirees and, after retirement, as "Mama Bear" for prisoners in high security confinement in Ohio. The doctor or nurse; the preschool, elementary school, or high school teacher, indeed the professor at a community college or working-class university; the priest, pastor or rabbi, each can present a similar skill and recognizable identity.

After all, why did Bob Moses leave Mississippi, or Stokely Carmichael leave Lowndes County, Alabama? At the same time that I acknowledge having known them and learned from them and admired them, I am constrained to point out that they were limited by coming from the North and having only the public identity of "organizer." Similarly Tom Hayden left Newark, Rennie Davis and Todd Gitlin left the Uptown neighborhood in Chicago. There were a few like Hollis Watkins and Curtis Hayes, who were from Mississippi, stayed on, and turned an initial commitment into an enduring presence and a way of life. But as a Movement, we didn't stay.

I am another instance of the same shortcoming. After coordinating Freedom Schools in Mississippi, I left the South for a teaching position at Yale, where I was miserable. Then, while living in Chicago before becoming a lawyer, I spent several years doing oral history, working for Saul Alinsky's school for organizers (the Industrial Areas Foundation Training Institute), and trying to find a solid and helpful way to contribute, not very successfully.

In Our Hands Is Placed a Power

Just as those seeking to practice accompaniment need a defined and publicly recognized way to do so, poor and working people need the daily experience of something different, something better. This "something different" was glimpsed in both the labor and civil rights movements.

The theme song of the modern trade union movement is "Solidarity Forever." Ralph Chaplin, a member of the Industrial Workers of the World, took the tune from "The Battle Hymn of the Republic" which in its turn had used the tune of "John Brown's Body." Just as Julia Ward Howe offered new words for a familiar tune to create "The Battle Hymn," so Chaplin devised new lyrics to make the song still ritually sung at union gatherings.

> In our hands is placed a power
> Greater than their hoarded gold,
> Greater than the might of armies
> Magnified a thousandfold.
> We can bring to birth a new world
> From the ashes of the old,
> For the Union makes us strong.
>
> Solidarity forever, solidarity forever,
> Solidarity forever, for the Union makes us strong.

Working people improvise their own forms of solidarity. A stubborn insistence on honoring the reality of what Stan Weir called the "family at work" lies behind the practice of disregarding seniority and dividing the available work equally during layoffs. Similarly countless rank-and-file movements have proposed that anyone who works full time for the union should earn no more than the highest-paid worker in the shop or office, and that such officers and "staffers" should return to the workplace after a fixed number of years. We must seek to discern such seeds of solidarity and nurture them.

Similarly in the South, during the civil rights movement of the 1960s, solidarity was sung forth and lived out. Old church hymns which affirmed that "I" would overcome some day gave way to freedom songs in which the protagonist was "we." In the song "I'm on My Way" the next to last verse cries out, "If you won't go/I'll go anyhow." But in the last verse we sang, "*We're* on our way/And *we* won't turn back."

SNCC's early style, writes Charles Payne, expressed "celebration of the potential of ordinary men and women, the desire to valorize as many voices as possible, rejection of individual celebrity, a striving for consensus, a disdain of credentials and hierarchy." The ordinary people with whom SNCC struggled to make a better world understood that "maintaining a sense of community was itself an act of resistance."[1]

I would add only that SNCC's early style was also internationalist. Soon after the bodies of James Chaney, Andrew Goodman, and Michael Schwerner were discovered, Bob Moses offered a few remarks at the site of the Mt. Zion Baptist Church in Philadelphia, Mississippi as part of an improvised occasion for remembering our three companions. The church had been burned to the ground after the deacons decided to make it available for a Freedom School. Chaney, Goodman, and Schwerner had gone to Philadelphia to find another location for the school. Bob might have been expected to speak only of matters internal to Mississippi and the civil rights movement. Instead he called attention to the Tonkin Bay incident that had just taken place, and affirmed a connection between what was happening to people of color in Mississippi and to people of color in Vietnam.

Howard Zinn, who was also present, remembered Bob Moses's commentary this way:

---

1. Payne, *I've Got the Light*, pp. 404–5.

Bob Moses spoke at the service, and we could see that his usual calm was missing. He held up that morning's newspaper from Jackson, and read the headline: "President Johnson Says 'Shoot to Kill' in the Gulf of Tonkin."

Bob spoke with a bitterness we were not accustomed to seeing in him. The government of the United States, he said, was willing to send armed forces halfway around the world for a cause that was incomprehensible, but it was unwilling to send marshals into Mississippi, though asked again and again, to protect civil rights workers from inevitable violence. And now three of them were dead.[2]

A year later, in August 1965, Bob Moses, David Dellinger, and several dozen others including me, white and black, were arrested as we sought to assemble on the steps of Congress to say that we were not at war with the people of Vietnam. A little later, SNCC endorsed draft resistance (a year before SDS did the same thing), and for this reason Julian Bond was at first denied the right to take his seat in the Georgia legislature. We sought to extend across national borders the fundamental affirmation that there is in every human being what Quakers call an "inner light."

Beyond individual actions, the task is to multiply opportunities to practice accompaniment, and patiently to create networks of new institutions. So many possibilities are available: for fellow workers, for students and their teachers, for clergy and their congregations, for neighbors experiencing hard times, for medical professionals and those who need their help.

Workers will create and recreate local unions because they need them, whatever may befall the national hierarchies that purport to enclose and represent them.

Collaborative learning will appear and reappear, whether among Brazilian landless laborers; workers seeking to make federal labor law a shield, if not a sword; children from whom stories of the ancestors have been wrongly withheld; or women anxious to escape preordained household roles.

Where two or three are gathered together in the name of bringing into being a world in which human beings share as members of one family, that world—so it was said of old—has already begun to exist.

---

2. Zinn, *You Can't Be Neutral on a Moving Train*, pp. 103–4.

Index

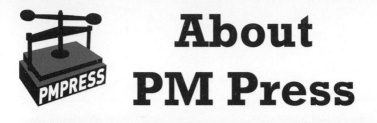

About
PM Press

politics • culture • art • fiction • music • film

PM Press was founded at the end of 2007 by a small collection of folks with decades of publishing, media, and organizing experience. PM Press co-conspirators have published and distributed hundreds of books, pamphlets, CDs, and DVDs. Members of PM have founded enduring book fairs, spearheaded victorious tenant organizing campaigns, and worked closely with bookstores, academic conferences, and even rock bands to deliver political and challenging ideas to all walks of life. We're old enough to know what we're doing and young enough to know what's at stake.

We seek to create radical and stimulating fiction and nonfiction books, pamphlets, t-shirts, visual and audio materials to entertain, educate, and inspire you. We aim to distribute these through every available channel with every available technology, whether that means you are seeing anarchist classics at our bookfair stalls; reading our latest vegan cookbook at the café; downloading geeky fiction e-books; or digging new music and timely videos from our website.

Contact us for direct ordering and questions about all PM Press releases, as well as manuscript submissions, review copy requests, foreign rights sales, author interviews, to book an author for an event, and to have PM Press attend your bookfair:

PM Press • PO Box 23912 • Oakland, CA 94623
510-658-3906 • info@pmpress.org

Buy books and stay on top of what we are doing at:

www.pmpress.org

MONTHLY SUBSCRIPTION PROGRAM

These are indisputably momentous times—the financial system is melting down globally and the Empire is stumbling. Now more than ever there is a vital need for radical ideas.

In the four years since its founding—and on a mere shoestring—PM Press has risen to the formidable challenge of publishing and distributing knowledge and entertainment for the struggles ahead. With over 200 releases to date, we have published an impressive and stimulating array of literature, art, music, politics, and culture. Using every available medium, we've succeeded in connecting those hungry for ideas and information to those putting them into practice.

Friends of PM allows you to directly help impact, amplify, and revitalize the discourse and actions of radical writers, filmmakers, and artists. It provides us with a stable foundation from which we can build upon our early successes and provides a much-needed subsidy for the materials that can't necessarily pay their own way. You can help make that happen—and receive every new title automatically delivered to your door once a month—by joining as a Friend of PM Press. And, we'll throw in a free T-Shirt when you sign up.

Here are your options:
- $25 a month: Get all books and pamphlets plus 50% discount on all webstore purchases
- $40 a month: Get all PM Press releases (including CDs and DVDs) plus 50% discount on all webstore purchases
- $100 a month: Superstar—Everything plus PM merchandise, free downloads, and 50% discount on all webstore purchases

For those who can't afford $25 or more a month, we're introducing *Sustainer Rates* at $15, $10 and $5. Sustainers get a free PM Press t-shirt and a 50% discount on all purchases from our website.

Your Visa or Mastercard will be billed once a month, until you tell us to stop. Or until our efforts succeed in bringing the revolution around. Or the financial meltdown of Capital makes plastic redundant. Whichever comes first.

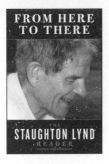

From Here to There
The Staughton Lynd Reader
Staughton Lynd • Edited with an
Introduction by Andrej Grubacic
$22.00 • 9x6 • 320 pages

From Here to There collects unpublished talks and hard-to-find essays from legendary activist historian Staughton Lynd.

The first section of the *Reader* collects reminiscences and analyses of the 1960s. A second section offers a vision of how historians might immerse themselves in popular movements while maintaining their obligation to tell the truth. In the last section Lynd explores what nonviolence, resistance to empire as a way of life, and working-class self-activity might mean in the 21st century. Together, they provide a sweeping overview of the life, and work—to date—of Staughton Lynd.

Both a definitive introduction and further exploration, it is bound to educate, enlighten, and inspire those new to his work and those who have been following it for decades. In a wide-ranging Introduction, anarchist scholar Andrej Grubacic considers Lynd's persistent concerns in relation to traditional anarchism.

Solidarity Unionism at Starbucks
Staughton Lynd and Daniel Gross
with illustrations by Tom Keough
$4.95 • 8.5x5.5 • 36 pages

Utilizing the principles of solidarity unionism, any group of co-workers can start building an organization to win an independent voice at work without waiting for a traditional trade union to come and "organize" them. Indeed, in a leaked recording of a conference call, the nation's most prominent union-busting lobbyist coined a term, "the Starbucks problem," as a warning to business executives about the risk of working people organizing themselves and taking direct action to improve issues at work.

Combining history and theory with the groundbreaking practice of the model by Starbucks workers, Lynd and Gross make a compelling case for solidarity unionism as an effective, resilient, and deeply democratic approach to winning a voice on the job and in society.

Wobblies and Zapatistas
Conversations on Anarchism, Marxism and Radical History
Staughton Lynd and Andrej Grubacic
$20.00 • 8x5 • 300 pages

Wobblies and Zapatistas offers the reader an encounter between two generations and two traditions. Andrej Grubacic is an anarchist from the Balkans. Staughton Lynd is a lifelong pacifist, influenced by Marxism. They meet in dialogue in an effort to bring together the anarchist and Marxist traditions, to discuss the writing of history by those who make it, and to remind us of the idea that "my country is the world." Encompassing a Left libertarian perspective and an emphatically activist standpoint, these conversations are meant to be read in the clubs and affinity groups of the new Movement.

The authors accompany us on a journey through modern revolutions, direct actions, anti-globalist counter summits, Freedom Schools, Zapatista cooperatives, Haymarket and Petrograd, Hanoi and Belgrade, "intentional" communities, wildcat strikes, early Protestant communities, Native American democratic practices, the Workers' Solidarity Club of Youngstown, occupied factories, self-organized councils and soviets, the lives of forgotten revolutionaries, Quaker meetings, antiwar movements, and prison rebellions. Neglected and forgotten moments of interracial self-activity are brought to light. The book invites the attention of readers who believe that a better world, on the other side of capitalism and state bureaucracy, may indeed be possible.

> "There's no doubt that we've lost much of our history. It's also very clear that those in power in this country like it that way. Here's a book that shows us why. It demonstrates not only that another world is possible, but that it already exists, has existed, and shows an endless potential to burst through the artificial walls and divisions that currently imprison us. An exquisite contribution to the literature of human freedom, and coming not a moment too soon."
> —David Graeber, author of *Fragments of an Anarchist Anthropology* and *Direct Action: An Ethnography*

Lucasville
The Untold Story of a Prison Uprising, 2nd edition
Staughton Lynd with a Foreword by Mumia Abu-Jamal
$20.00 • 8.5x5.5 • 256 pages

Lucasville tells the story of one of the longest prison uprisings in United States history. At the maximum security Southern Ohio Correctional Facility in Lucasville, Ohio, prisoners seized a major area of the prison on Easter Sunday, 1993. More than 400 prisoners held L block for eleven days. Nine prisoners alleged to have been informants, or "snitches," and one hostage correctional officer, were murdered. There was a negotiated surrender. Thereafter, almost wholly on the basis of testimony by prisoner informants who received deals in exchange, five spokespersons or leaders were tried and sentenced to death, and more than a dozen others received long sentences.

Lucasville examines the causes of the disturbance, what happened during the eleven days, and the fairness of the trials. Particular emphasis is placed on the inter-racial character of the action, as evidenced in the slogans that were found painted on walls after the surrender: "Black and White Together," "Convict Unity," and "Convict Race."

An eloquent Foreword by Mumia Abu-Jamal underlines these themes. He states, as does the book, that the men later sentenced to death "sought to minimize violence, and indeed, according to substantial evidence, saved the lives of several men, prisoner and guard alike." Of the five men, three black and two white, who were sentenced to death, Mumia declares: "They rose above their status as prisoners, and became, for a few days in April 1993, what rebels in Attica had demanded a generation before them: men. As such, they did not betray each other; they did not dishonor each other; they reached beyond their prison 'tribes' to reach commonality."

> "*Lucasville* is one of the most powerful indictments of our 'justice system' I have ever read. What comes across is a litany of flaws deep in the system, and recognizably not unique to Lucasville. The detailed transcripts (yes, oral history!) give great power to the whole story."
> —Howard Zinn, author of *A People's History of the United States*

Labor Law for the Rank and Filer
Building Solidarity While Staying Clear of the Law, 2nd edition
Staughton Lynd and Daniel Gross
$12.00 • 8x5 • 120 pages

Have you ever felt your blood boil at work but lacked the tools to fight back and win? Or have you acted together with your co-workers, made progress, but wondered what to do next? If you are in a union, do you find that the union operates top-down just like the boss and ignores the will of its members?

Labor Law for the Rank and Filer: Building Solidarity While Staying Clear of the Law is a guerrilla legal handbook for workers in a precarious global economy. Blending cutting-edge legal strategies for winning justice at work with a theory of dramatic social change from below, Staughton Lynd and Daniel Gross deliver a practical guide for making work better while re-invigorating the labor movement.

Labor Law for the Rank and Filer demonstrates how a powerful model of organizing called "Solidarity Unionism" can help workers avoid the pitfalls of the legal system and utilize direct action to win. This new revised and expanded edition includes new cases governing fundamental labor rights as well as an added section on Practicing Solidarity Unionism. This new section includes chapters discussing the hard-hitting tactic of working to rule; organizing under the principle that no one is illegal, and building grassroots solidarity across borders to challenge neoliberalism, among several other new topics. Illustrative stories of workers' struggles make the legal principles come alive.

> "As valuable to working persons as any hammer, drill, stapler, or copy machine, *Labor Law for the Rank and Filer* is a damn fine tool empowering workers who struggle to realize their basic dignity in the workplace while living through an era of unchecked corporate greed. Smart, tough, and optimistic, Staughton Lynd and Daniel Gross provide nuts and bolts information to realize on-the-job rights while showing us that another world is not only possible but inevitable."
> —John Philo, Legal Director, Maurice and Jane Sugar Law Center for Economic and Social Justice